Labrador Love

A Comprehensive Guide to Care, Communication, and Adventures with Your Loyal Companion

From Labrador Retriever Origins to Training and Health: Everything You Need to Know to Forge a Deep Connection with Your Dog

By Max Walker

A Comprehensive Guide to Care, Communication, and Adventures with Your Loyal Companion

Copyright © 2023 Daring LTD

All rights reserved. No part of this book may be reproduced, stored in a retrieval system, or transmitted in any form or by any means, electronic, mechanical, photocopying, recording, or otherwise, without the prior written permission of the author, except for brief excerpts used for review purposes.

The information contained in this book has been collected with the utmost care and precision. However, the authors and publishers assume no responsibility for any errors, omissions, or damages resulting from the use of the information contained herein. It is always advised to consult a veterinarian or qualified expert for the specific needs of your Labrador.

The names of products, trademarks, logos, and service marks mentioned in this book are the property of their respective owners. The use of such names, trademarks, and brands does not imply any affiliation or endorsement by them.

Every effort has been made to ensure that the images and illustrations used in this book are authorized and properly credited. However, if you recognize any improperly attributed image or illustration, please contact us for the necessary corrections.

Please note that the personal experiences and testimonials mentioned in this book are based on the individual experiences of Labrador Retriever owners and do not guarantee similar results or success.

Special thanks to all those who contributed to the creation of this book, including experts, veterinarians, breeders, and Labrador Retriever enthusiasts. Without their support and contributions, this project would not have been possible.

Thank you for choosing to read "**Labrador Love: A Comprehensive Guide to Care, Communication, and Adventures with Your Loyal Companion**". We hope that this book provides you with the information and inspiration needed to enjoy the wonderful companionship of your Labrador.

For inquiries, permissions, or questions, please contact:

daring.limited@gmail.com

Author: Max Walker   Illustrator: Nassy Art   **Publisher:**

A Comprehensive Guide to Care, Communication, and Adventures with Your Loyal Companion

CONTENT

PREFACE 6

AUTHOR'S NOTE 7

CHAPTER 1 - UNVEILING LABRADOR'S ORIGINS: FROM NEWFOUNDLAND TO BELOVED COMPANION 8

CHAPTER 2 - LABRADOR BREED STANDARDS: UNVEILING THE PERFECT CANINE FORM 11

    GENERAL APPEARANCE 11

    CHARACTERISTICS 11

    TEMPERAMENT 11

    HEAD AND SKULL 11

    EYES 12

    EARS 12

    MOUTH 13

    NECK 13

    FOREQUARTERS 13

    BODY 14

    HINDQUARTERS 15

    FEET 15

    TAIL 15

    GAIT AND MOVEMENT 16

    COLOR 16

    SIZE 17

    COAT 17

    DEFECTS 18

CHAPTER 3 - ABILITIES 20

    HUNTING DOG 20

    GUIDE DOG FOR THE BLIND 20

    GUIDE DOG FOR PEOPLE WITH DISABILITIES 21

    HEARING GUIDE DOG 22

    SEARCH AND RESCUE DOG 22

    WATER RESCUE DOG 23

    DRUG-DETECTION DOG 23

    ANTITERRORISM DOG 24

    COMPANION DOG 24

CHAPTER 4 - THE LABRADOR'S CHARACTER: A HEART OF GOLD 26

CHAPTER 5 - LABRADOR HABITS: UNDERSTANDING THE CANINE LIFESTYLE 29

CHAPTER 6 - COMMUNICATING WITH YOUR FRIEND 30

    WHAT IS THE PURPOSE OF 30

COMMUNICATION 30

THE MESSAGES OF THE MUZZLE 30

BODY AND TAIL LANGUAGE MESSAGES 31

HOW TO COMMUNICATE WITH THE DOG IN WORDS 32

WHEN THE DOG BARKS WITHOUT 33

APPARENT REASON 33

OLFACTORY SIGNALS AND TERRITORY MARKING 33

WHEN THE DOG "POOPS" IN THE HOUSE . 34

COMMUNICATION RULES 34

CHAPTER 7 - LABRADOR REPRODUCTION: THE JOURNEY OF PARENTHOOD 36

MATING 36

    CHOOSING THE RIGHT PARTNER 36

    PLANNING THE MATING 37

    PREPARING THE ENVIRONMENT 38

    MONITORING MATING 38

    PREGNANCY 39

    THE BIRTH 39

    TAKING CARE OF THE PUPPIES 41

    FALSE PREGNANCY 41

    UNDESIRED MATING 41

CHAPTER 8 - CHOOSING THE PERFECT LABRADOR: FINDING YOUR IDEAL COMPANION 42

THE VISIT TO THE BREEDING FARM 43

WHEN TO ACQUIRE IT 44

MALE OR FEMALE 45

BLACK, YELLOW OR CHOCOLATE 45

CHAPTER 9 - BREEDING A PUPPY 47

PUPPY FEEDING 47

HEALTH 48

LEGAL OBLIGATIONS 48

FIRST DAY WITH YOUR PUPPY 49

PHYSICAL ACTIVITY 50

CHAPTER 10 - CARING FOR YOUR LABRADOR: NURTURING A HEALTHY AND HAPPY PET 51

COAT 51

TEETH 51

EYES 52

EAR CARE 52

Nail trimming 52

CHAPTER 11 - FEEDING YOUR LABRADOR: A BALANCED DIET FOR OPTIMAL HEALTH 54

ENERGY 56

NUTRIENTS 57

    CARBOHYDRATES OR GLUCIDES: 57

    FATS OR LIPIDS: 57

    PROTEINS: 57

    MINERAL SALTS: 58

FOODS 58

    MEAT: 58

    OFFAL: 58

    FISH: 58

    EGGS: 59

    MILK: 59

A Comprehensive Guide to Care, Communication, and Adventures with Your Loyal Companion

FATS, LARD, AND VEGETABLE OILS: 59
CEREAL FLAKES AND PUFFED RICE: 59
VEGETABLES AND FRUIT: 59
BONES: 59
SWEETS AND CHOCOLATE: 59

READY-MADE FOODS 59
SIMPLE FOODS: 60
COMPLETE FOODS: 60
COMPLEMENTARY FOODS: 60

CHAPTER 12 - HEALTH AND HYGIENE 61

CHAPTER 13 - COMMON LABRADOR DISEASES: PREVENTION AND MANAGEMENT 62
ORGANIC DISEASES 62
INFECTIOUS DISEASES 62
INFESTING DISEASES (PARASITOSIS) 66
MYCOSIS 66
CONGENITAL DISEASES 66
HEREDITARY DISEASES 66

CHAPTER 14 - FIRST AID FOR LABRADORS: KEEPING YOUR CANINE SAFE AND HEALTHY. 68

EMERGENCIES SHOCK 69

POISONINGS 69
INSECT STINGS 69
SNAKEBITE 70
HEATSTROKE 70
FRACTURES 70

FIRST AID TIPS 71
SYMPTOMS OF SERIOUS ILLNESSES 71
GENERAL SYMPTOMS OF ILLNESS 71

HOW TO MEASURE BODY TEMPERATURE 71
HOW TO MEASURE HEART RATE 71
WHAT TO KEEP FOR EMERGENCIES 71
HOW TO BEHAVE WITH A TRAUMATIZED DOG 71
HOW TO TRANSPORT A TRAUMATIZED DOG 72
HOW TO DEAL WITH A WOUND 72
INJURIES TO EYES, EARS, NOSE 72
BURNS 73
FREEZING 73
CHOKING 73
CONVULSIVE AND EXCITATORY CRISES ... 73
HOW TO ADMINISTER MEDICATIONS 74
MEDICATIONS FOR PARENTERAL USE 74
MEDICATIONS FOR EAR INFECTIONS 74
DRUGS FOR EYES 74
SUPPOSITORIES 74

CHAPTER 15 - OUTDOOR ADVENTURES WITH YOUR LABRADOR 76

CHAPTER 16 - TRAINING TIPS AND TRICKS FOR A HAPPY LABRADOR FAMILY 77
BASIC OBEDIENCE 77
HUNTING TRAINING 80

CHAPTER 17 - DOG SHOWS 83
PREPARATION FOR SHOWS 84
THE FIRST TIME 84
THE CLASSES 85

A Comprehensive Guide to Care, Communication, and Adventures with Your Loyal Companion

PREFACE

The book "**Labrador Love: A Comprehensive Guide to Care, Communication, and Adventures with Your Loyal Companion**" is a comprehensive manual on training, care, and health for your four-legged friend. This detailed guide begins with the breed's origins, describing the breed standards, general appearance, and characteristics of Labrador Retrievers, along with their attitudes and talents, making them ideal companions for hunters, the visually impaired, the handicapped, and rescuers.

The book continues with a section dedicated to communicating with your Labrador Retriever, examining the messages of the muzzle, body, and tail, verbal language, and the dog's olfactory signals, as well as common behaviors such as barking and "marking" territory.

Next, the guide focuses on Labrador Retriever breeding, offering advice on choosing the right partner, planning mating, preparing the environment, and caring for puppies.

The Labrador Retriever health section covers legal obligations, general care, nutrition, nutritional principles and foods, as well as organic, infectious, and infesting diseases that can affect your dog.

"The Complete Guide to Labrador Retrievers" is aimed at those who are interested in learning about this dog breed in depth, from origins to attitudes, health to training. It is aimed at Labrador Retriever owners or those who intend to become owners, dog trainers, veterinarians, and anyone

Pic- 01-Efe_Madrid

who loves dogs and wants to know more about their care and well-being.

In recent years, dog breeding has undergone a considerable transformation; the number of people who feel the need or desire to have a dog, especially a breed, increases every year. The dog is no longer seen exclusively as an aid in certain functions, but primarily as a friend to spend leisure time with and live a different experience, with a close human-animal relationship.

Labrador is a breed that has all the morphological and behavioral characteristics to be widely spread. It is necessary to learn more about these dogs, who can be useful not only for hunting but also in many other uses, and are excellent companions for humans.

A Comprehensive Guide to Care, Communication, and Adventures with Your Loyal Companion

AUTHOR'S NOTE

Welcome to the book **"Labrador Love: A Comprehensive Guide to Care, Communication, and Adventures with Your Loyal Companion."** This book has been created with the intention of providing readers with a complete and in-depth guide to all things related to Labrador Retrievers, one of the most beloved dog breeds in the world.

Before embarking on this journey of discovering Labradors, I want to emphasize that the information contained in this book is based on my experience and thorough research. However, it is important to understand that each dog is a unique individual, and experiences may vary from one animal to another. Therefore, it is always advisable to consult a veterinarian or qualified expert for the specific needs of your Labrador.

Furthermore, this book is not intended as a substitute for professional advice. The information provided here is for educational and informational purposes. While we have made every effort to provide accurate and up-to-date information, we cannot take responsibility for any errors or omissions that may occur. It is always recommended to verify information with reliable sources and make informed decisions based on the individual needs of your Labrador.

This book is divided into several chapters, each exploring a specific aspect of Labrador life. From the historical origins of the breed to selecting the perfect dog, from care and nutrition to managing health and common issues, each chapter is designed to provide a comprehensive and detailed overview of the different facets of life with a Labrador.

I hope this book provides you with the information and resources needed to better understand your Labrador, take care of them, and build a lasting and fulfilling bond. Remember, love and commitment are essential in maintaining a safe and happy environment for your Labrador, and our goal is to provide you with the basic knowledge to do so to the best of your ability.

I would like to thank everyone who contributed to the creation of this book, including industry experts, veterinarians, breeders, and Labrador Retriever enthusiasts. Without their generosity of time, knowledge, and experiences, this project would not have been possible.

Enjoy reading, and may your journey into the world of Labradors be filled with joy, love, and knowledge!

Max Walker

A Comprehensive Guide to Care, Communication, and Adventures with Your Loyal Companion

CHAPTER 1 - UNVEILING LABRADOR'S ORIGINS: FROM NEWFOUNDLAND TO BELOVED COMPANION

This chapter will take you back in time to discover the historical roots and fascinating origins of the Labrador Retriever. This extraordinary breed has a deep connection to the region of Newfoundland and Labrador in Canada, and its history is intertwined with the work of fishermen and a passion for retrieving.

This chapter will explore the birth of the breed, its original role as a working dog, and its success as a beloved family companion worldwide.

As happens with many other dog breeds, opinions and theories about the origins of Labrador Retrievers are controversial. The currently predominant hypothesis indicates the island of Newfoundland as the place of origin for these dogs.

Descriptions by travelers from the early 19th century attest to the existence of dogs with characteristics similar to those of Labradors used by fishermen on the coasts of Newfoundland in Canada. It seems that these dogs descended from hunting dogs brought to those places by settlers who resided in the ports of Newfoundland during the fishing season and who shuttled between Canada and Great Britain with fishing boats loaded with cod.

Contrary to what its name suggests, the Labrador does not come precisely from the Canadian region of Labrador. It seems, in fact, that the predecessors of this dog came rather from the coasts of Newfoundland, and it is not known how this denomination was arrived at. In reality, the two areas are geographically very close, and initially, the two terms Newfoundland and Labrador were used indiscriminately to indicate those particular dogs that were then used by cod fishermen on the coasts of Newfoundland.

What is certain is that the Labrador Retriever as a well-defined breed was born in the UK thanks to the passion and skill of English breeders of the late 19th and early 20th centuries. The dogs of St. John, as they were called at that time, were used both for hunting and for retrieving lines at sea because they were excellent swimmers.

There are English sources that testify to how this type of dog was born from crosses between the large Newfoundland dog and smaller hunting dogs similar to Pointers. This type of mating was intended to "build" more agile subjects, with shorter hair, and with a better sense of smell than the Newfoundland dog itself.

What is certain is that it was the particular environment in which these dogs had to live that allowed the selection of those characters of robustness and resistance that the Labrador still possesses today. The climate of those areas undoubtedly contributed to the selection of the thick, waterproof coat. The physical characteristics of these animals, described with usually black coat, corresponded to those of a short-haired dog, not too big and very fast on land and in water.

The St. John water dog, ancestor of the Labrador, was described in 1814 by Colonel Hawker as "an excellent dog for any type of hunting, usually black-coated and not larger than a Pointer. It is extremely fast in running and swimming; it has beautiful legs, short hair, and the tail is not as curly as that of the Newfoundland dog".

There are depictions of the St. John's Dog with slightly more curly hair and tail compared to today's Labrador, but overall they are quite similar. In fact, at that time there was not yet a clear distinction between the two current breeds, Newfoundland and Labrador, and the two terms were often used interchangeably. The breed was probably imported to England in the mid-19th century through fishing vessels that shuttled between the island of Newfoundland, where cod was fished along its coasts, and the ports of Poole in Dorset and Clidas in Scotland. However, it is unclear how stable the breed's traits were at that time. According to English breeders, who were knowledgeable about selection rules, it is unlikely that fishermen had already selected the completely black coat or the particular attractive qualities that the Labrador currently possesses. Most likely, there were dogs with fairly varied morphology, and the selection made, of course, empirically, by fishermen probably only concerned their ability to work and their physical resistance to bad weather. Another theory suggests that Labrador dogs originated from the coastal areas of northern Portugal, called Castro Laborieri dogs. It is a breed that still exists today, actually resembling an unattractive Labrador, which according to some, could have been imported into England through maritime traffic between the two countries. However, this hypothesis is less accepted by experts. The gentlemen of the late 19th century, passionate hunters, selected retriever breeds to combine the typical pointing ability of Setters or Pointers with the "specialists" in retrieval activity. What is certain is that the more recent history of these dogs is all English. In fact, the ancient passion of this people for dogs is well known, which has always been dedicated to breeding and selecting the most disparate canine breeds. It seems that, thanks to their qualities, the ancestors of Labradors were immediately noticed by English breeders and used to strengthen the bloodlines of retriever dogs. Their intention was to add trained fetching dogs alongside pointing dogs. This is how the first Labradors began to be selected, although there was still confusion with Newfoundland. In an article in the Illustrated London News in 1870, which reports observations on the Birmingham dog show, there is a comment on Newfoundland dogs that says: "It would be desirable to see them divided into two classes: the Newfoundland we already know and the carbon black Labrador, which is undoubtedly another breed." One of the first great ancestors we know was a dog selected by Lord Malmesbury named Buccleuch Avon, born in 1885. Lord Malmesbury donated some descendants of his dog to other passionate hunting nobles, and between the end of the 19th century and the beginning of the 20th century, all the current characteristics of the Labrador retriever were established. Other important figures in the history of selecting these dogs were Colonel Peter Hawker, the first writer of the St. John's Dog, Lord Knutsford, Lord Home, and the Duke of Buccleuch. In England, there were only ten double champions, that is, both beauty and work champions, and they all descended from three Lord Malmesbury stallions: Avon, Netherby Boatswain, and Smiler. The Kennel Club officially recognized the breed in 1904, and the breed association was founded in 1916. The Best in Show award at the

famous Crufts show in England was awarded to a Labrador for two consecutive years: 1932, 1933; the champion was Bramshaw Bob, bred by Countess Lorna Howe. Among the people who contributed significantly to the formation of the breed, the most important was Mrs. Gwen Broadley, who worked...

Among the people who contributed significantly to the formation of the breed, Mrs. Gwen Broadley was very important. Working on the foundations laid by Lady Howe, she produced dogs of great class and excellent temperament. One cannot talk about Labradors without mentioning the Sandyland kennel prefix, which produced more than seventy champions for the breed.

Initially, Labradors were predominantly black, but gradually, the recessive yellow coat began to be selected for as well. The credit for founding the association for yellow Labradors goes to Mrs. Veronica Wormald in 1925.

The breed began to spread initially mainly in English-speaking countries, such as the United States, where it was officially recognized in 1917, and then in many other countries. The breed standard was first drafted by English breeders in 1887, then established in 1916 by the newly formed club, and updated after the Second World War.

A Comprehensive Guide to Care, Communication, and Adventures with Your Loyal Companion

CHAPTER 2 - LABRADOR BREED STANDARDS: UNVEILING THE PERFECT CANINE FORM

These standards provide a guide for assessing the ideal structure and characteristics of the dog, ensuring that Labradors maintain their distinctive features. This chapter will explore the conformation criteria of Labradors, from anatomical details to coat characteristics, giving you a comprehensive overview of the breed standards.

The breed standard represents the set of morphological and character traits that the "ideal dog" should possess. These characteristics, in fact, allow it to perform the function for which it was selected at its best. However, it is an abstract description that does not correspond to any particular subject. It represents the "yardstick" to which canine experts must refer to evaluate animals that are submitted to their judgment but, even more so, the guide for breeders in selecting their dogs. The Labrador Retriever standard was drafted in the country of origin of the breed, that is, by the English Kennel Club. It is classified in this way by international cynology: FCI n. 122 of July 5, 1988.

GENERAL APPEARANCE

The appearance of the Labrador should be that of a solid and compactly built dog; very active. With a broad skull, wide and deep chest, well-rounded ribs, broad and powerful loins and hindquarters. The coat should be close, short, with a dense undercoat and without fringes.

As a hunting dog, the Labrador must possess qualities of robustness and endurance that allow it to work in adverse weather conditions on all types of terrain; in particular, it must be a good swimmer to retrieve ducks and other waterfowl.

CHARACTERISTICS

Very agile dog, of good character, possesses an excellent sense of smell, a great passion for water, and easily adapts to any environment. Faithful companion.

TEMPERAMENT

Intelligent, exuberant and at the same time docile. Eager to please and of a friendly nature, with no trace of aggressiveness. Should not be excessively timid. When evaluating a Labrador, in addition to their physical characteristics, some behavioral aspects must also be taken into account as they make for a good retrieving dog with a very typical temperament. A beautiful dog with character defects will also be penalized in beauty shows. They must have an unsurpassed sense of smell, a friendly and lively personality, and a true passion for water. They are a very intelligent dog that, despite their unrestrained playfulness, is easily trainable.

HEAD AND SKULL

The head and skull of the Labrador Retriever are distinctive and important characteristics of the breed. The Labrador Retriever's skull is wide and square, with a straight forehead and a broad upper jaw that forms a right angle with the skull. The head

A Comprehensive Guide to Care, Communication, and Adventures with Your Loyal Companion

of the Labrador Retriever should be proportionate to the rest of the body, with a balanced and harmonious shape.

According to the official Labrador Retriever standard, the dog's skull should be wide and square, with a straight forehead and a broad upper jaw. The cheeks should be well-filled and spaced apart from the upper jaw. The stop should be well-defined, but not excessive. The ears should be attached high on the skull and hang downward, with rounded tips.

In general, the head and skull of the Labrador Retriever should be in harmony with the rest of the body and meet the needs of the breed, which has been selected to be an efficient and athletic retrieving dog.

The Labrador Retriever has a broad skull with a pronounced stop; parallel cranial-facial axes; a clean head with dry, fleshy cheeks that are not too thick; medium-length, powerful, and non-cutting jaws; a broad nose with well-developed nostrils. The characteristics of the head are centered around the function it must perform in retrieving; the muzzle should be wide, the jaws strong and well-developed in order to carry even quite heavy birds. Overall, the head should give the impression of power and roundness without being too short and massive. The nose also plays a fundamental role; the nose should be broad with wide nostrils and in line with the nasal bridge. The stop, that is the step between the nose and the forehead, should be very pronounced, with a clear break. The muzzle is parallel to the head line.

EYES

The Labrador Retriever is a medium-sized dog with an intelligent and benevolent expression. The coat color is brown or hazel. Eyes that are too light in color are considered a fault. The eyes should have fairly pronounced eyebrows and should not protrude. The pigmentation of the eye contributes greatly to the beauty of the gaze, which is why eyes that are too light, as sometimes happens in dogs with a chocolate-colored coat, are undesirable. The eyelids should be close-fitting and free of abrasions. Overall, the eyes of the Labrador Retriever should be healthy and function properly, with a cheerful and affectionate expression that reflects the breed's friendly and playful personality.

EARS

The Labrador Retriever's ears are attached high on the skull and hang down towards the bottom, with rounded tips. They should not be large and heavy, but rather hang close to the head and be slightly set back. The eyes and ears need to be well-protected to allow the dog to work in dense vegetation.

The ears should not be too large and heavy but sufficiently developed to protect the ear canal from air and water. The Labrador Retriever's ears should be soft and flexible, with a wide surface area of attachment that allows the dog to hear sounds with great precision. According to the official Labrador Retriever standard, the dog's ears should be attached high on the skull and hang down towards the bottom, with rounded tips. In general, the Labrador Retriever's ears should be in harmony with the dog's head and skull and meet the needs of

A Comprehensive Guide to Care, Communication, and Adventures with Your Loyal Companion

the breed, which was selected to be an efficient and athletic retrieving dog.

MOUTH

The mouth should be strong and well-shaped, with healthy and regular teeth that fit together perfectly. The Labrador Retriever's bite should be scissors, which means that the upper and lower teeth fit together perfectly. This type of bite is particularly important for a retrieving dog, as it allows them to grasp and hold the game without damaging it.

According to the official Labrador Retriever standard, the dog's mouth should be well-proportioned and equipped with strong and regular teeth. The bite should be scissors, with well-aligned and interlocking teeth. The gums should be healthy and light pink.

In general, the Labrador Retriever's mouth should be able to function effectively and meet the needs of the breed, which has been selected to be an efficient and athletic retrieving dog.

Strong jaws and teeth, scissors bite with regular and complete teeth inserted perpendicular to the jaws. Evaluating the relationship between the two dental arches, scissors closure is when the inner face of the upper incisors touches the outer face of the lower incisors. A tenacious closure is when the margins of the incisors coincide. In both cases, the length of the two jaws, the upper and the lower, is equal.

The presence of prognathism (when the jaw is shorter than the mandible) and overbite (when the jaw appears shorter than the mandible) are considered defects. The Labrador should have a scissors bite. In America, however, the standard calls for a tenacious closure.

NECK

Clean, strong and solid, well inserted on the shoulders. The morphology of the Labrador Retriever's neck is one of the most distinctive characteristics of the breed. The neck is strong, straight and well-proportioned to the rest of the body, and widens slightly at the base to connect with the shoulders. The neck should be long enough to allow the dog to retrieve game without difficulty, but not so long as to compromise the body's balance.

According to the official Labrador Retriever standard, the dog's neck should be well-modeled and long enough to allow the dog a good grip on game, but not so long as to impede its balance and mobility. The skin of the neck should be soft and free of wrinkles.

In general, the morphology of the Labrador Retriever's neck should be in harmony with the rest of the body and meet the needs of the breed, which has been selected to be an efficient and athletic retriever.

FOREQUARTERS

Long and oblique shoulders, good bone structure. From the elbow to the ground, the legs are straight both when viewed from the side and from the front. The front legs of the Labrador Retriever are robust and strong, designed to support the weight of the body and assist the dog during running and swimming. The front legs of the Labrador Retriever should be straight and parallel, with elbows close to the body and strong, muscular shoulders.

According to the official Labrador Retriever standard, the dog's front legs should be straight and parallel, with elbows close to the body and strong, muscular shoulders. The shoulders should be well sloped, with a moderate angle that allows the dog to have a fluid and powerful movement. The bones of the front legs should be robust and strong, with oval paws and well-tucked toes.

In general, the front legs of the Labrador Retriever should be designed to support the weight of the body and assist the dog during running and swimming. This morphology of the front legs is important to ensure that the Labrador Retriever is able to perform the physical activities for which it has been selected, such as retrieving and swimming.

The alignment of a leg is determined by the direction of its bone rays with respect to the considered horizontal ground. Considering the dog in profile, the vertical line dropped from the scapula-humeral joint should touch the ground at the tip of the toes. If the foot is positioned further back from this vertical line, the dog is said to be "underneath" or "thrown forward" in front. If the foot is positioned further forward than the vertical line, the dog is said to be "out in front" or "overreaching". The latter defect is very rare.

In the Labrador, the slope of the shoulder is very important; the scapula should form an angle of 45° with the horizontal line and an angle of 90° with the humerus. From the elbow down, the leg should be perfectly straight both when viewed from the front and in profile.

Additionally, legs that are too close together are incorrect as they indicate poor development of the pectoral muscles. The opposite defect is also penalized, as legs should not be excessively spaced apart.

Two other defects that can sometimes be observed in the front legs are "pigeon-toed" and "splayfoot". Pigeon-toed front legs are characterized by inwardly rotated feet and elbows "loose" from the chest; splayfoot is the opposite defect, where feet are rotated outward and elbows are too close to the chest.

BODY

The Labrador Retriever has a broad and deep chest with well-developed pectoral muscles that allow him to swim. However, the chest should not be too wide as it would create excessive resistance in the water. From above, the chest area appears wide due to the curvature of the "barrel" ribs, which give the breed its characteristic shape.

The back of the Labrador Retriever should be short and straight, with a flat topline that runs from the head to the kidneys without interruption. The loins should be strong and compact, while the kidneys should be large and well-developed.

Overall, the Labrador Retriever's body should be sturdy and well-proportioned, designed to support the weight of the body and assist the dog during running and swimming. This body structure is important to ensure that the Labrador Retriever can perform the physical activities for which it was selected, such as retrieving and swimming.

A Comprehensive Guide to Care, Communication, and Adventures with Your Loyal Companion

HINDQUARTERS

Well developed. The croup does not slope down towards the tail. Well-angled hocks. Well-descended hocks. Cow hocks should be avoided. The hindquarters of the animal are of utmost importance, as they transmit the propulsive impulse to the trunk during movement. The hind limb, in addition to being well angled at the knee, should have good musculature on both the thighs and the buttocks. Possible defects of perpendicularity essentially consist of canines (internally rotated limbs) or, conversely, in cow hocks where the hocks are rotated internally while the feet are rotated outwards. Overall, the hindquarters should be slightly wider than the front. The hind legs of the Labrador Retriever are sturdy and strong, designed to support the body weight and assist the dog during running and swimming. The hind legs of the Labrador Retriever should be straight and parallel, with strong and muscular knees. According to the official Labrador Retriever standard, the hind legs of the dog should be straight and parallel, with strong and muscular knees. The thighs should be strong and muscular, with robust calves supporting the powerful movements of the dog. The hind paws should be oval and tightly knit, with toes tightly knit and short and robust nails. In general, the hind legs of the Labrador Retriever should be designed to support the body weight and assist the dog during running and swimming.

FEET

The feet of the Labrador Retriever are large and sturdy, designed to support the body weight and assist the dog during running and swimming. According to the official Labrador Retriever standard, the dog's feet should be round and tightly knit, with toes tightly knit and short and robust nails. The toes should be well spaced and rounded, with a horny nail that protects the toes during physical activities. The feet should be strong and muscular, with good blood circulation that helps maintain body temperature during physical activities. In general, the feet of the Labrador Retriever should be designed to support the body weight and assist the dog during running and swimming. Round, compact, with well-arched phalanges and well-developed pads. Labrador feet have been described as "webbed" because they should facilitate the dog's swimming. However, one should not think of a "duck" foot. A correct foot is round and well arched, not flat or with open toes; the skin of the interdigital spaces is well developed, but the spaces themselves should not be visible. Neither the excessively small cat foot nor the hare foot, which is long and oval, are correct.

TAIL

The tail of the Labrador Retriever is a distinctive feature of the breed and should be long and strong, with good musculature. The tail should be well set at the base, with moderate length varying from the base to the tip.

According to the official standard of the Labrador Retriever, the dog's tail should be long and strong, with good musculature. The tail should be well set at the base and have moderate length varying from the base to the tip. The tail should be carried low when the dog is at rest and lifted when the dog is active or excited. The tail should be able to move freely and curl evenly upon itself.

 A Comprehensive Guide to Care, Communication, and Adventures with Your Loyal Companion

It should be thick at the base, tapering gradually towards the tip; of medium length, entirely covered with short, dense hair, without fringes, giving it the appearance of an otter's tail. It can be carried merrily, but never curled over the back.

The typical tail has a wide base and gradually tapers towards the tip: it is very important as it serves as a rudder during retrieving.

The main faults are:

Tail too thin;

Tail curled at the end;

Tail set on too high;

Tail with fringes.

It can be carried high, especially in young dogs, but must maintain its typical otter-like conformation. It is almost always in motion.

In general, the Labrador Retriever's tail is an important indicator of the dog's mood and attitude. The tail's morphology is important to ensure that the Labrador Retriever can effectively communicate with its owner and other animals.

GAIT AND MOVEMENT

The gait and movement of the Labrador Retriever are important characteristics that define its morphology and breed standard. The breed is known for its agility and smooth, powerful gait, making it suitable for many sports and work activities.

The ideal gait of the Labrador Retriever is an agile, decisive, and powerful gallop that adapts to its athletic nature. The dog should have excellent movement technique, with hind limbs that push strongly and forelimbs that lift evenly. The dog's back should be straight and rigid, with good musculature and a wide range of motion at the hips.

The movement of the Labrador Retriever should be smooth and powerful, with good flexibility and efficient movement technique. The dog should have excellent coordination, with limbs moving in harmony to ensure a decisive gait and good stability.

In general, the gait and movement of the Labrador Retriever are important characteristics that define its morphology and breed standard. These characteristics make the dog suitable for many sports and work activities, such as retrieving and swimming.

COLOR

A Comprehensive Guide to Care, Communication, and Adventures with Your Loyal Companion

Pic-12

Pic-13

Black, yellow, or brown (liver or chocolate). Yellow can range from light cream to fox red. A small white spot on the front of the chest is allowed.

Originally, the Labrador was black in color. It seems that in 1899, a yellow puppy appeared for the first time from parents that were both black. Initially, this coat color was considered outside of the standard, and the puppies were euthanized as atypical. Later, fortunately, the existence of the yellow coat was also recognized. The third coat color of the Labrador, currently defined as "chocolate," was initially called "liver."

It is a very beautiful burnt brown color but difficult to achieve, especially with very homogeneous characteristics. The first chocolate champion, Cookridge Tango, was bred by Mrs. Pauling. Marjorie Seatterwhite raised under her prefix Lawnswood the dog Hot Chocolate, the only English and American champion of this color.

SIZE

The size of the Labrador Retriever is an important characteristic that defines its morphology and breed standard. According to the American breed standard, males should have a height at the withers between 56 and 58 cm, while females should be between 51 and 56 cm. The ideal weight for males is between 29 and 36 kg, while for females it is between 25 and 32 kg.

American Labradors are slightly larger than those found in Europe, such as the English Labrador, where the standard for males is 57.5-62 cm and for females is 55-60 cm. The size of the Labrador Retriever should be proportionate, with a good bone structure and well-developed musculature. The dog should have a strong and muscular build, with adequate shoulder width and a balanced trunk length in relation to the height at the withers.

Overall, the size of the Labrador Retriever is an important characteristic that defines its morphology and breed standard. This size is suitable for many sports and work activities, such as retrieving and swimming, and makes the dog a reliable and versatile companion.

COAT

The coat of the Labrador Retriever is an important and distinctive characteristic of the breed that defines its morphology and breed standard. The coat should be smooth and uniform, with medium length and good density. The fur is short and dense without wavy fringes, rather rough to the touch, and resistant to weather conditions.

The breed standard provides for the coat to be black, brown, or yellow. The black color should be uniform and shiny black, without shades or spots. The brown color should be uniform and dark brown, without shades or spots. The yellow color should be uniform and golden yellow, without shades or spots.

The coat of the Labrador Retriever is weather-resistant and water-resistant, making it suitable for outdoor activities and swimming. It should be well-groomed and free of knots or tangles, with good quality and texture.

Overall, the coat of the Labrador Retriever is an important characteristic that defines its morphology and breed standard. This durable and uniform coat makes the dog a reliable and versatile companion for many outdoor activities.

Males should have two normally-sized testicles that have descended into the scrotum.

Currently, as has happened with other breeds, there is an increasingly marked separation between working and show lines of dogs, so it is possible to see Labradors that are very different from each other, especially with regard to size. However, it is desirable that this trend does not go beyond acceptable limits in order to avoid forgetting the origins and true aptitudes of this splendid breed.

DEFECTS

Anything that deviates from the breed standard is considered a defect. Serious defects include: prognathism (a condition in which the lower jaw protrudes compared to the upper jaw. This can cause an abnormal appearance of the muzzle and can affect the dog's ability to chew and swallow properly. In some cases, prognathism can also interfere with the dog's ability to breathe normally. This condition can be caused by genetic or environmental factors) or enognathism (a condition opposite to prognathism, in which the upper jaw protrudes compared to the lower jaw. This can cause an abnormal appearance of the muzzle and can affect the dog's ability to chew and swallow properly. In some cases, enognathism can also interfere with the dog's ability to breathe normally), lack of undercoat, wavy fur and fringes on the tail, defective movement, pointed muzzle, large and heavy ears, cow hocks and tail carried curled over the back.

Understanding these criteria will help you assess the conformation of your Labrador and gain a better understanding of its structure and distinctive characteristics. Remember that breed standards serve as a reference point to ensure the preservation of the ideal qualities of Labrador Retrievers as both working and companion dogs.

A Comprehensive Guide to Care, Communication, and Adventures with Your Loyal Companion

Pic - 02

A Comprehensive Guide to Care, Communication, and Adventures with Your Loyal Companion

CHAPTER 3 - ABILITIES

The Labrador is considered one of the most versatile breeds ever selected. It's not by chance, in fact, that in addition to its highly appreciated hunting qualities, this breed has also conquered a prominent place in various other fields.

As the ultimate retriever, it possesses a formidable instinct which, combined with its remarkable learning ability, makes it an exceptional hunting dog. In addition to hunting, there are numerous other uses in which the Labrador has proven to be excellent, thanks also to the ease and enthusiasm with which it learns:

HUNTING DOG

The Labrador Retriever is a breed that was originally selected to be a hunting dog. This breed is very intelligent and easy to train, making it an excellent choice for many hunting activities.

In particular, the Labrador Retriever is very popular as a retriever hunting dog. These dogs are very skilled at retrieving birds and other wild animals that have been shot during the hunt. Their affectionate nature and love of play make them particularly suited for this type of work, as they are highly motivated to work and retrieve the trophy for their owner.

In addition to retrieving, Labrador Retrievers can also be trained to assist with other hunting activities, such as game tracking and tracing. These dogs are very skilled at teamwork and following their owner's commands, making them an excellent choice for many hunting activities.

Ultimately, the Labrador Retriever is a very popular and versatile hunting dog, thanks to its intelligence and love of work. This breed is well suited to many hunting activities, such as retrieving, game tracking, and tracing, making it an excellent choice for many hunters.

GUIDE DOG FOR THE BLIND

It is particularly suited to this work because of its natural characteristics, such as its intelligence, reliability, and protective instinct. Additionally, this breed is also very gentle and affectionate, which makes it highly appreciated by its owners. This is an activity in which it has been successfully employed for several years. Its balanced

A Comprehensive Guide to Care, Communication, and Adventures with Your Loyal Companion

temperament is perfect for the role of a guide dog for the blind: it must not be distracted by anything or anyone during its work, must not be aggressive as it must be able to be in any type of environment in contact with people or other dogs. It is also important for the social life of the blind that it attracts attention for its beauty and does not inspire fear in others.

Generally, at six months of age, the puppy destined to become a guide dog is entrusted to a trainer who raises it in the family for another six months. During this period, the puppies learn to face all kinds of situations in everyday life: they enter shops, offices, and all public places, learn to walk without fear in traffic and socialize with people even in crowded environments. Once a month, they are checked by specialized instructors from the school who monitor their progress. At twelve months, the puppies are returned to the training center for further training. Here, they are rigorously tested for character and health. Only after passing this selection are the chosen dogs ready to start the real five-month course. This training includes specific guide training, such as learning verbal commands to avoid obstacles, follow safe routes, and other necessary skills to help their owner navigate safely.

Once trained, guide dogs can provide great support and safety to blind people, allowing them to be more independent and lead a fuller and more active life. Guide dogs are an important resource for many blind people, and their contribution to the quality of life of the visually impaired cannot be overstated.

GUIDE DOG FOR PEOPLE WITH DISABILITIES

The Labrador, along with other retrievers, has proven to be extremely useful in helping people with physical disabilities by substituting themselves for them in various activities to overcome their daily difficulties.

Dogs trained for this particular purpose can perform up to fifty different commands: helping their owners dress and undress, opening and closing doors, taking objects and bringing them to their owners, picking up items, helping with grocery shopping, and much more.

Additionally, assistance dogs can also help reduce anxiety and depression, increase their owners' security and confidence, and provide them with lovely and reliable companionship. In this case, just as with the blind, the psychological support that a person gains from having a faithful companion always nearby is crucial.

The Labrador Retriever is one of the most suitable breeds for this work due to its intelligence, reliability, and sweetness. Moreover, this breed is also very affectionate and friendly, making it much appreciated by its owners.

A Comprehensive Guide to Care, Communication, and Adventures with Your Loyal Companion

Just like guide dogs for the blind, assistance dogs for people with disabilities must also undergo rigorous training to learn the tasks they will have to perform. This training can last from several months to several years, depending on the complexity of the tasks the dog must learn.

Ultimately, the use of an assistance dog like the Labrador Retriever can have a significant positive impact on the quality of life of people with disabilities, providing them with a reliable source of support and companionship.

HEARING GUIDE DOG

The Labrador Retriever is also used as a hearing guide dog for deaf or hard-of-hearing people. These dogs are trained to alert their owners to important sounds such as the phone ringing, doorbell, fire alarm, and other sounds that may be dangerous or important for safety.

Guide dogs for non-hearing people are trained to respond to visual signals instead of sounds, such as a hand gesture or a nod of the head. This means that their owners can be alerted to important sounds without having to hear them directly.

Just like guide dogs for the blind and assistance dogs for people with disabilities, hearing guide dogs must also undergo rigorous training. This training can last for several weeks or months and involves learning specific visual signals and the ability to respond to them reliably.

The Labrador Retriever is one of the most suitable breeds for this work due to its intelligence, reliability, and sweetness. Moreover, this breed is also very affectionate and friendly, making it much appreciated by its owners.

Ultimately, the use of a hearing guide dog like the Labrador Retriever can help improve the quality of life of non-hearing people, providing them with a reliable source of alert for important sounds and increasing their safety and independence.

SEARCH AND RESCUE DOG

The Labrador Retriever is also employed in the search for missing or lost persons. These dogs are trained to follow the scent tracks of missing people and provide information to rescue workers about their location.

Search dogs are trained to follow specific scent tracks, such as those of a missing person's skin or clothing scents, and to detect any smells of decomposition or other sources of danger. In some cases, search dogs can also be trained to indicate the presence of a living or deceased person with a specific behavior, such as barking or sitting.

The Labrador Retriever is one of the most suitable breeds for this work due to its excellent sense of smell and its intelligent and reliable nature. Moreover, this breed is also very affectionate and friendly, making it much appreciated by its owners.

A Comprehensive Guide to Care, Communication, and Adventures with Your Loyal Companion

In conclusion, the use of a search dog like the Labrador Retriever can help increase the chances of finding missing persons and provide crucial information to rescue workers, ultimately helping to save lives.

WATER RESCUE DOG

Pic-7 by Dean - Unsplash

The Labrador Retriever is also a very useful dog for water rescue. This breed is known to be an excellent swimmer and has a strong inclination towards water work, making it ideal for this type of task.

Water rescue dogs are trained to find and retrieve people who have fallen into the water or have been swept away from shore. These dogs can also be used to rescue people involved in water accidents or to recover floating objects or bodies.

To become a water rescue dog, a Labrador Retriever must undergo rigorous training that includes learning to swim, searching for objects or people in the water, and working collaboratively with its human handlers to perform rescues. These dogs must also be able to work in difficult and potentially dangerous conditions, such as strong currents or cold water, and must be strong and resilient enough to swim long distances.

Labradors often accompany the better-known Newfoundland dogs as they are also excellent swimmers and have no fear of water. They have the advantage of having short fur that does not allow people to grab onto them as they do with Newfoundlands, but this lack is compensated for by the use of a special harness with handles.

In conclusion, using a Labrador Retriever for water rescue can be very helpful in saving human lives and preventing water accidents, especially in emergency or difficult situations. These dogs can make a difference between life and death in many situations and are highly appreciated and respected for their courage and dedication to their work.

DRUG-DETECTION DOG

The Labrador Retriever is also a very common breed for use as a drug-detection dog.

These dogs are trained to detect the presence of drugs, such as marijuana, cocaine, heroin, and other illegal substances, and can be used in many different contexts, including airports, schools, public offices, and other public places.

The training process for a drug-detection dog involves teaching the dog to recognize the odor of drugs and to signal their presence to its human handlers. This training can be very rigorous and may take months or even years to complete.

Once a drug-detection dog is trained, it can be used in many different ways to help prevent the spread of drugs and ensure the safety of the community. For example, a drug-detection dog can be used to check luggage at the airport or to inspect vehicles entering and leaving a school or public office.

Drug-detection dogs are initially trained to find a toy in increasingly difficult hiding places. Subsequently, the odor of drugs is associated with the toy so that they become accustomed to searching for objects with that odor. The idea that dogs are drugged to get them addicted to drugs is a myth.

In conclusion, using a Labrador Retriever as a drug-detection dog can be very helpful in preventing the spread of drugs and ensuring the safety of the community. These dogs are very well trained and can work in many different situations, making them a very popular option for this type of task.

ANTITERRORISM DOG

The Labrador Retriever is also a commonly used breed as an anti-terrorism and explosive detection dog. These dogs are trained to detect the presence of explosive substances such as dynamite, tritium, and other similar substances, and can be used in many situations to ensure public safety.

The training process for an anti-terrorism and explosive detection dog involves teaching the dog to recognize the smell of explosive substances and to signal their presence to their human handlers. This training can be very rigorous and can take months or even years to complete.

Once an anti-terrorism and explosive detection dog is trained, it can be used in many different situations to ensure public safety, such as inspecting vehicles entering and exiting a public event or checking luggage at the airport.

Ultimately, the use of a Labrador Retriever as an anti-terrorism and explosive detection dog is an important contribution to public safety. These dogs are very well trained and can work in many different situations, making them a very popular choice for this type of task.

COMPANION DOG

The Labrador Retriever is also very popular as a companion dog. This breed is known for its sweet, affectionate, and friendly temperament, which makes it an ideal companion for many people. Labrador Retrievers are very active and playful, but at the same time, they are also very relaxed and calm, which makes them perfect for indoor living.

As a companion dog, the Labrador Retriever is very versatile and can adapt to many different life situations. They can be kept in apartments or houses with a garden, depending on the owner's preferences. They are also very active and need a lot of physical exercise, so owners must be ready to provide them with many opportunities to explore and play.

The Labrador Retriever is also very intelligent and easy to train, making it a great companion dog for people looking for an animal that can learn quickly and participate in many activities with them. These

A Comprehensive Guide to Care, Communication, and Adventures with Your Loyal Companion

dogs are also very affectionate and friendly with children, making them a great choice for families.

Despite not having the size of a lap dog, it is considered an ideal companion for both single people and families, as it gets along well with children, plays willingly, is docile, and does not bark often.

In conclusion, the Labrador Retriever is a very popular companion dog for many reasons. Its friendly and playful personality, intelligence, and versatility make it an ideal companion for many people and families.

In summary, I would describe this breed as "eclectic" in its functions and attitudes; the only field where it is really a "failure" is that of guard and defense, as by nature it would not harm a fly: it has its size and tone of voice, which can intimidate those who do not know it, but in reality, it does not know what it means to attack or bite a person.

CHAPTER 4 - THE LABRADOR'S CHARACTER: A HEART OF GOLD

The character of the Labrador is one of its most distinctive and beloved traits. These dogs are known for their affectionate, joyful, and loyal personality, which makes them perfect as family companions and loving pets. Let's delve further into the characteristics that define the character of a Labrador.

Labradors are renowned for their immense capacity to love and bond with people. They are extremely affectionate and deeply desire to be an integral part of the family. They are often described as dogs who love cuddles and are always ready to receive and give affection.

Labradors have a gentle and patient nature, especially with children. They are known to be tolerant and patient even when treated clumsily or playfully by little ones. This makes Labradors a popular choice for families with children.

Intelligence and eagerness to learn: Labradors are intelligent dogs and have a strong desire to please their owners. They are known for their quick learning abilities and are inclined towards training. This makes them easy to handle and suitable for a variety of activities such as agility, search and rescue work, and service dog training.

One of the distinctive traits of a Labrador is their affinity for water. They are passionate water dogs and love swimming, playing, and cooling off in water puddles. This characteristic stems from their origins as retriever dogs in Newfoundland and their waterproof coat.

Labradors are known for their infectious cheerfulness and zest for life. They are always ready to play, run, and have fun. Their positive energy and optimistic attitude make them joyful companions and a source of great entertainment.

Labradors are sensitive dogs and attuned to the emotions of their owners. They deeply desire to please and tend to seek approval and gratification from the humans they are bonded with.

A dog with a strong, lively, and at the same time, lovable temperament: it lives very well in a group and, although a hierarchy is necessarily established, it is difficult not to reach agreement within it. Similarly, it lives in harmony with any living being: dog, cat, horse, etc. In particular, it loves to be with people, it is extremely sociable with anyone who pays it the slightest attention and does not spare parties for anyone.

On the other hand, it hates solitude but will adapt patiently if left alone. However, if you have to be away for long periods during the day, you will have to think about providing it with company. The ideal would be another dog, perhaps of the same age, with whom it can play. Sometimes you can see totally undisciplined dogs that cannot be in environments with other dogs or people because they are too excited and create chaos. This happens to animals that grow "alone", perhaps free in a splendid park but

 A Comprehensive Guide to Care, Communication, and Adventures with Your Loyal Companion

deprived of the relationship with humans. In these cases, the fault lies solely with the owners since it would be enough to live a little more with the dog to accustom it to the "life of society" and transform it into a faithful and inseparable companion.

Given its good character, it will never protest too much if left alone, but breeders believe that it is a dog destined for constant contact with people.

It is an expansive dog and shows it at all times. This festivity of his can sometimes be excessive since he often does not seem to realize his strength and size. For this reason, it is necessary to accustom him to control his bursts of affection from an early age. A big Labrador that, taking a run, places his powerful paws on a person's chest can sometimes be misunderstood in his intentions.

Numerous owners, whether it was their first dog or they had already had others, have said they never want another breed again.

The Labrador is a dog that makes its presence felt, it is fun, has a distinct personality, and is affectionate. Generally, it does not choose a single person as its owner within the family. It becomes attached and willingly stays with all members, just as it is happy when a stranger arrives. It is a dog that rarely barks to defend the territory; guard duty is absolutely not included in its habits. Rather, it barks to invite another dog or person to play, barks to ask for something, but if a stranger entered his house, he would greet and compliment him as if he had known him forever.

Despite its size and its "aquatic" habits that lead it to throw itself into any body of water or puddle that comes under its aim, it is a dog that can be kept comfortably at home, extraordinarily clean and composed.

Despite being very exuberant, once the first stages of wild joy when someone arrives or when he "greets" his owner have passed, the Labrador generally gets used to behaving correctly at home. Generally, it crouches at the owner's feet and stays there without disturbing. It needs constant contact with the owner and must be taken out as often as possible. In this way, you will notice that the more you stay with the dog, communicate with him through gestures, expressions, and tones of voice, the deeper the relationship of mutual understanding becomes. You will reach the point where even without speaking, the dog will understand your intentions, and on your part, you will learn to know the dog's "language" that constantly communicates its needs to you.

Remember that he loves being with you and will easily adapt wherever you take him. Don't worry about his size; often a big Labrador crouched under a restaurant table is much less bothersome than a pocket-sized dog that can't sit still for a moment.

A Comprehensive Guide to Care, Communication, and Adventures with Your Loyal Companion

One of the fundamental traits of the breed, which is also emphasized in the standard, is the total absence of aggression. There are few situations in which it is acceptable for a Labrador to show its teeth. It may happen between two males, but even then, such behavior should be discouraged in every way.

A Labrador should never growl at a person unless deliberately threatened or frightened by an unusual attitude or dress, but even in this case, aggression should manifest discreetly.

If well-treated, a Labrador is a naturally "happy" dog and shows it on every occasion with its exuberance and vitality. At any moment, unless it is sleeping, its beautiful tail is in motion. Instinctively, it is a friendly dog that loves people, and consequently, it makes itself loved. A very effective definition of this breed is that of the "eager-to-please" dog. A Labrador is happy when it does something for its owner, and the only reward it requires is a friendly pat or a "good boy." It is a dog that loves to be useful, be active, and obey its owner. The worst thing that can be done to one of these dogs is to leave it alone in idleness. It is then that it will start to cause disasters, not out of spite but out of boredom.

It is important to emphasize that, although the traits described above are common in most Labradors, each dog will have their own unique personality. Some Labradors may be more timid or reserved, while others may be more outgoing and lively. It is crucial to respect and understand the different nuances of character in each individual dog.

 A Comprehensive Guide to Care, Communication, and Adventures with Your Loyal Companion

CHAPTER 5 - LABRADOR HABITS: UNDERSTANDING THE CANINE LIFESTYLE

Understanding the habits and natural instincts of this breed will help you build a strong relationship and meet your dog's needs. Many of these points will be further explored in the upcoming chapters.

Socialization and interaction:

- The sociable nature of Labradors and their natural inclination towards human and canine interactions. How to promote proper socialization from a young age to ensure balanced and friendly behavior.

- Recommended socialization activities for your Labrador, including encounters with other dogs, positive experiences with people, and exposure to different environments. These experiences contribute to a confident and adaptable personality.

- Games that typically engage Labradors and keep them busy, such as object retrieval, swimming, and interaction with interactive toys. Learn how to stimulate your Labrador through play and keep them mentally and physically active. Play helps strengthen the bond between you and your Labrador, creating mutual trust and fun.

- Proper meal planning for your Labrador, including choosing a balanced diet and managing portions. How to meet your dog's nutritional needs to maintain good health.

- Typical eating habits of Labradors, such as the tendency to eat quickly or be food-driven. Manage these habits to prevent overweight issues or digestive disorders.

- Labrador grooming, including regular brushing, occasional baths, and nail care. Learn the best practices to keep your dog's coat clean and healthy.

- The importance of dental hygiene for Labradors and how to maintain proper teeth cleaning to prevent dental problems and bad breath.

- The importance of regular exercise for Labradors and discover recommended activities to satisfy their need for movement, such as walks, interactive games, and sports activities.

- The importance of providing your Labrador with adequate rest and sleep, creating a comfortable environment and a regular resting routine.

Understanding your dog's habits will help you create a happy and fulfilling environment for them, promoting their overall health and well-being.

A Comprehensive Guide to Care, Communication, and Adventures with Your Loyal Companion

CHAPTER 6 - COMMUNICATING WITH YOUR FRIEND

Everyone has noticed the variety and diversity of signals that dogs use in encounters with both other dogs and humans: vocal signals, such as whining, barking, growling, or visual signals, such as lowering their front paws to "invite play," keeping their ears and tail lowered in a position of "fear," or wagging their tails, shaking their whole body, in anticipation of some tasty treat or a nice walk. All these signals, and many others, such as olfactory signals, transmitted mainly by urinating, are part of a kind of language, which is then the characteristic "communication system" of each species, in the sense that within each species animals communicate with their own messages.

Tail signals could be a tool for social or sexual signaling, as it covers or uncovers the anogenital area, hiding or showing it to others to stimulate attention. Or a tool for signaling the "social rank" of the individual within the group-pack, as the intensity and amplitude of the wagging can indicate the level of control of the animal's emotions.

WHAT IS THE PURPOSE OF COMMUNICATION

Obviously, the transmission of signals involves a certain degree of sociality, that is, the development of a social life within which each individual finds their place, their rank, and their role in relation to others. And this is advantageous both for the individual and for the group; in fact, the first can better find through the indications of others, the possibility of feeding and mating, that is, of surviving and reproducing, while the second can maintain its cohesion without its members constantly fighting each other. In addition, communication between members of the social group allows for better defense against dangers, which are also promptly signaled at a distance, especially through acoustic messages. The dog belongs to a highly social species and as such is rich in communicative signals, especially visual, acoustic, and olfactory ones.

THE MESSAGES OF THE MUZZLE

The expressions of the muzzle, or the so-called facial mask, are fundamental in the language of the dog, especially in those breeds that have the possibility of modifying the position of the ears. The different positions of the ears, together with those of the lips, can reveal the dog's intentions. In summary, we can assume that:

fixed and attentive gaze with narrowed pupils, perhaps accompanied by a muffled growl and a slight raising of the hair on the back, are signs of threat;

lowered and evasive gaze usually indicates shyness, but attention, if it enters a state of real fear, it can progressively become a signal of pre-attack;

attentive gaze, accompanied by tail wagging, barking, and the front of the body lowered, can mean: "do you want to play with me?";

languid gaze and, "humanly" speaking, almost pleading, perhaps with the body in a "sit" position, with a little drool dripping from the mouth, means that our friend is patiently waiting for the long-awaited meal!

"absent" gaze, apathetic position and little reaction to the signals we transmit, can indicate that

A Comprehensive Guide to Care, Communication, and Adventures with Your Loyal Companion

"something is wrong" at the organic level, that there may be a pathology of various kinds, or even a nervous pathology; there are cases where such a gaze is concomitant with real nervous "crises," which can also involve episodes of sudden and absolutely unpredictable aggression, even directed towards people that the animal knows well, even the owner.

BODY AND TAIL LANGUAGE MESSAGES

Interpreting a dog's body and tail language messages is an important skill to better understand the dog's emotions and intentions. Here are some common things to consider:

The meaning of wagging the tail is not entirely clear yet. We all know how to pick up the message when our dog comes towards us wagging its tail, with a bark, a bowl or a ball in its mouth, and interpret it as a desire to go for a walk or to receive the long-awaited meal or play with us.

TAIL UP: A raised tail can indicate that the dog is happy and confident. However, if the tail is stiff, it could also signal defensive behavior or a dominant attitude.

TAIL WAGGING: A tail wagging rapidly can indicate that the dog is excited or anxious. Often, the dog wags its tail, perhaps in a more rigid and less relaxed way, even when in a situation of rivalry with other dogs or showing aggression. The fact is that this behavior already manifests itself in the puppy during suckling or when there is competition with littermates. With the movement of the tail, therefore, each subject can signal its presence since by wagging, the dog spreads its own olfactory signal around, which, as we will see later, is another very important communication system. Wagging in anticipation of play or a reward is also a childish signal that the adult dog maintains towards its peers and humans.

TAIL DOWN: A tail that goes down could indicate that the dog is scared or insecure.

Tail between the legs: A tail that hides between the dog's legs can indicate fear or submission, the intention on the part of the dog to declare itself submissive, lost, or even "in love" in the case of a male courting a female in heat.

EARS: A dog's ears can say a lot about its emotions. If they are upright, the dog may be vigilant or interested, while if they are lowered, it may be scared or insecure.

BODY POSITION: A dog's body posture can provide indications of its intentions. For example, a dog that crouches may be ready to play, while a dog that stands up may be ready to defend itself.

As a whole, the dog's entire body is capable of transmitting signals, both by changing postures and by raising its fur, so much so as to make it seem larger in size.

The general principle is simple: the more imposing the animal's figure appears (upright ears, fur standing on the back, upright posture), the more it can signal its state of dominance over the surrounding environment, including other dogs or people in it; the more the figure appears "shrunken."

In general, it is important to consider the context in which the dog is and its overall behavior to correctly interpret its messages. In addition, every dog has a unique personality, so it is useful to know your own dog and learn to interpret its individual signals.

Che cosa dice il cane quando abbaia o emette suoni

Messages or "vocalizations" are widely used by dogs to communicate even at a considerable distance. Barking and other sounds emitted by a dog can say a lot about its emotions and intentions. Here are some common things to consider:

Short and intense barking: This type of barking can indicate that the dog is alert or is alerting the owner to something that it believes is out of place. We all know well the chorus of barks that can erupt at the most unexpected times, when, in the utmost tranquility, in the middle of our well-deserved nighttime sleep, dogs from all over the neighborhood signal to each other that a suspicious noise has been heard nearby or, simply, that someone is passing in front of a gate.

Prolonged barking: This type of barking can indicate that the dog is bored, frustrated, or in need of attention. However, this is one of the purposes of acoustic communication, to signal a danger to the group, so that it can prepare for defense.

Continuous barking: Often, it signals to the owner that someone is knocking at the door, which is natural as a defense system of the animal to protect its territory, but quite annoying, often, for the owner himself and his neighbors. This type of barking can indicate that the dog is scared, anxious, or annoyed.

Whining: This low, guttural sound can indicate that the dog is scared or anxious. The puppy signals to the mother, with plaintive whines, that it is cold, hungry, or in need of care.

Growling: This threatening sound can indicate that the dog is defensive or dominant.

Sighing: This sound can indicate that the dog is relaxed and at ease.

As with body language messages, it is important to consider the context in which the dog is in and its overall behavior to correctly interpret its sounds. Furthermore, every dog has a unique personality, so it is useful to know your dog and learn to interpret its individual signals.

HOW TO COMMUNICATE WITH THE DOG IN WORDS

Communication with your dog is essential to establish a relationship of trust and harmony. Here are some tips for communicating with your dog:

• Learn the dog's signals: observe how your dog behaves when he is happy, nervous, hungry, or tired, and try to respond accordingly.

• Use body language: the dog's body language, such as tail position, facial expression, and movement, is an important means of communication. Learn to interpret your dog's signals and use your body language to communicate with him.

• Talk to your dog: speak to your dog using a calm and reassuring tone of voice. This will help create an empathic connection with your animal and communicate better.

• Use verbal commands: teach your dog basic commands such as "sit," "stay," "come," and "no."

A Comprehensive Guide to Care, Communication, and Adventures with Your Loyal Companion

Use them consistently and repeat them often so that your dog can learn them well.

• Reward positive behavior: reward your dog when he behaves as desired, such as when he correctly follows a command. This will help reinforce positive behavior and improve communication between you.

Remember that every dog is a unique individual and may require time and patience to understand its way of communicating. The important thing is to be consistent and constant in communicating with your animal.

The dog learns to associate a certain signal from us with its behavior and subsequently with our response. For example, it can associate the word "come" with approaching us and being rewarded with a delicious treat. Or the word "sit" with sitting in front of us and immediately receiving a pat on the head and a "good boy!" Or even the word "off!" with its attempt to climb onto our favorite couch, followed by a sharp "no!" of disapproval. Through these associations, what is called "conditioning learning" is established, meaning the dog learns that there is a relationship between a certain auditory signal, its response behavior, and what follows, especially if it is a reward.

The corresponding signal word for each message we want to convey can be of any type, the important thing is that for each message, the same word is used, said with the same tone of voice and accompanied by the same gestures, otherwise our Labrador will become "confused," and we cannot expect it to obey different signals that mean the same thing!

WHEN THE DOG BARKS WITHOUT APPARENT REASON

It often happens that our friend literally tries to "make us deaf" with its persistent barking, and it also happens to hear desperate owners saying, "I don't know what to give him or what to say to make him stop barking." Now, if we consider that barking is really a system of communication, it is a logical consequence to expect that our prompt attention and immediate response to the message will not only not inhibit it, but rather increase it. It is therefore up to the owner to distinguish between correct barking and annoying, useless, or inappropriate barking, paying attention to the former and ignoring the latter, so that even the animal can distinguish when this communication system is approved or not. For example, if it barks persistently after bringing us the ball, we should not think that it will stop playing with it, because it will promptly bring it back and start barking again. If, on the other hand, we teach it to obey a command that makes it be quiet, then as a reward, we can throw the ball far away to let it play!

OLFACTORY SIGNALS AND TERRITORY MARKING

Why do pee breaks never end? Especially if we have a male dog, we will certainly have noticed that, during the daily walk, if there are other male or female dogs in heat, especially if we recall it in an unfamiliar environment, it is his duty to "mark" all the vertical objects present with urine: trees, car wheels, corners of buildings, etc. In this way, our dog "signals" to others that it is in that place and, possibly, does not mind mating with available females. The olfactory message is based on the emission of odors through urine, feces, saliva, and directly from specific glands; during heat periods, so-called "pheromones" are also emitted, secretions with a particular odor that indicates readiness to mate.

Territory marking is more intense from "dominant" animals, to "make room" for themselves against the "submissive," especially of the same sex. Such behavior can be partially reduced by castration. Often, digging holes in the ground can also be a system of "territory marking."

WHEN THE DOG "POOPS" IN THE HOUSE

The presence of this annoying behavior is characteristic in a newly introduced puppy in the household environment and gradually diminishes until it disappears when the animal, following proper training by the owner, has "learned" to only "poop" outside the home environment. If this behavior persists, it may be an indication of either a pathological state (the dog is sick and unable to hold it), inadequate training, or various forms of "behavioral disorder," such as "separation anxiety" if the dog only poops in the house when left alone. A particular case is "submission urination": the dog emits small or large amounts of urine, for example, when we return home after leaving him alone for a longer or shorter period during the day, or when he is scolded even just verbally, or when he is particularly agitated.

This is an emotional phenomenon that almost never resolves with punitive measures: as in the previous cases and in all other "behavioral problems," it is essential to thoroughly investigate the causes that have determined them. Once it is excluded that the problem depends on some particular organic disease, it is possible to intervene with an appropriate methodology to modify the animal's behavior in a possibly lasting and definitive way.

COMMUNICATION RULES

The dog is a "social" animal; its behaviors are determined both by its species and breed characteristics and by the environment in which it lives and evolves over time, from when it is a puppy until it is an adult. Therefore, to impose proper education to obtain a balanced and non-neurotic animal, it is important to start communicating with him and understanding his messages precisely when he is a puppy because it is mainly in the first period of life that he has the maximum learning capacity.

• If you want to "subdue" the puppy or the adult (assuming that you have previously established your "dominance" over him), take him by the "scruff of the neck," as the mother does with her own puppies. Looking directly at a dog's eyes is a signal of "challenge."

• Some particular stimuli, such as hats, uniforms, suits, or unusual clothing, as well as the veterinarian's lab coat, can cause avoidance or sometimes aggression in an unaccustomed dog.

Sometimes the dog may also react negatively to apparently neutral stimuli, at least to our eyes. Usually, this happens because the animal associates such stimuli with particularly negative or traumatic experiences he had previously.

• One should not approach a stranger's dog with raised arms or gesticulating animatedly or stomping one's feet.

A Comprehensive Guide to Care, Communication, and Adventures with Your Loyal Companion

Every obedience "command" should be given with a consistently same acoustic and visual message. It is important, if the dog is "managed" by various family members, that all give consistent signals and have the same reactions to his behaviors.

• Rewards or punishments (not too violent!) can be effective only if given immediately after the animal's behavior and not if they are given hours or even minutes later. Communication between the child and the dog is usually very immediate and mutually valid; however, it is advisable to control, especially initially, the approaches between the two, to avoid unpleasant misunderstandings on both sides.

A Comprehensive Guide to Care, Communication, and Adventures with Your Loyal Companion

CHAPTER 7 - LABRADOR REPRODUCTION: THE JOURNEY OF PARENTHOOD

Breeding Labrador Retrievers is a fascinating and important topic to understand for those looking to deepen their knowledge of this breed or venture into breeding themselves. In this chapter, we will explore in detail the Labrador's reproduction process and the wonderful experience of parenthood.

Female Labradors typically reach sexual maturity around 6-12 months of age. During the reproductive cycle, also known as estrus or heat, hormonal fluctuations occur, preparing the female's body for the possibility of pregnancy.

Choosing the right mate is a crucial step in the Labrador breeding process. It is important to select a healthy, high-quality male that possesses desirable traits to preserve and enhance the breed. Careful breeders consider factors such as pedigree, physical conformation, temperament, and genetic profile to ensure a good combination of traits in the offspring.

Once the mate is selected, mating usually occurs naturally, allowing the dogs to establish a bond and increase the chances of successful breeding. Pregnancy lasts an average of 63 days, during which the female requires special care and attention to ensure her and the developing puppies' health.

Labrador delivery can be an intense experience, but most females handle it naturally. It is important to be prepared to assist the mother during the process and provide a safe and comfortable environment for the birth of the puppies. After delivery, the mother takes care of her pups, providing warmth, milk, and necessary care for healthy growth.

Once born, the puppies require careful nurturing and proper socialization. This includes vaccinations, proper nutrition, basic training, and exposure to various experiences and people to promote the development of a well-balanced and social Labrador.

While breeding Labrador Retrievers can be a rewarding experience, it is important to consider the ethical aspects and the responsibility it entails. Acting in accordance with the ethical guidelines of responsible breeders is crucial, ensuring the health and well-being of the parents and puppies, and working towards breed improvement in line with breed standards.

MATING

The breeding of Labrador Retrievers should be carefully planned to ensure the health and well-being of the dogs and their puppies. The choice of the most suitable mating should be made with great care and with specific knowledge derived from adequate basic preparation and good experience. If you are not sufficiently prepared, it is advisable to rely on the advice of experienced and reliable breeders. It is necessary to evaluate not only the individual subjects but also to know the genealogies and the results of previous matings.

Below, read carefully the advice, rules to follow, and important information to know.

CHOOSING THE RIGHT PARTNER

Ensure that the chosen dog is in good health and temperament and does not have genetic or behavioral problems. Check the health of the dogs:

A Comprehensive Guide to Care, Communication, and Adventures with Your Loyal Companion

before mating, both the male and female should undergo medical exams to ensure they do not have diseases or genetic problems. The breeding dogs must be healthy and should not transmit inherited abnormalities (hip dysplasia, cryptorchidism, ectropion, entropion, deafness, blindness, progressive retinal atrophy, and others). They must also present adequate morphological characteristics and a frank and well-balanced character.

PLANNING THE MATING

Choose the right time for mating based on the female's heat cycle. Avoid mating the female too young or too old.

But how to detect heat?

• It lasts about 3 weeks with significant individual variations.

• The behavior of the bitch changes: it becomes nervous and irritable with frequent and unpredictable attempts to escape and overcome obstacles, looking for males.

• She plays willingly with other dogs, both males and females, and even with the owners, showing signs of mating.

• She urinates very frequently, but only a few drops at a time, and often raises one of her hind legs like a male.

• The vulva swells, and the bitch licks herself frequently.

• There are slight bloody vaginal secretions for the first 9-10 days.

• Ovulation occurs between the 10th and 14th day, and the female accepts the male. However, there is wide individual variability.

The first heat usually occurs between 8 and 12 months, but it is recommended to let the bitch be covered starting from the second or third heat, as the body often has not yet completed its growth, and therefore, pregnancy could compromise normal bodily development. Heats occur throughout the female's life, as she does not undergo menopause, and therefore, they do not stop with age.

It is a good practice not to mate the female every heat but every other heat, allowing sufficient time between one pregnancy and another. After 7-8 years, it is good practice not to mate females anymore. The various physiological moments of the reproductive cycle are influenced by complex hormonal variations. The female accepts the male exclusively during the estrus period, generally between the 10th and 14th day, although some females accept the male for several days, and others for a very short period: one day or even less. Once fertilization has occurred, the female generally no longer accepts the male. The best time for mating can be identified through microscopic examination of a vaginal smear or through analysis of blood progesterone.

Males also reach sexual maturity between 8 and 12 months, but it is recommended to let them accompany females only after a year. They are attracted by the odor emitted by females that they can perceive even at considerable distances. The male is fertile throughout his life, if kept active, while if a dog has never mounted before 4-5 years, it will be difficult to reproduce it.

A Comprehensive Guide to Care, Communication, and Adventures with Your Loyal Companion

Dogs are a monomestrous species, in which heat and ovulation occur on average every six months, but with wide variability (5-12 months) due to both individual and seasonal factors. Wild canids generally come into heat only once a year.

PREPARING THE ENVIRONMENT

Create a comfortable and safe environment for mating. Make sure the dogs feel at ease. It is important that the female understands where she needs to give birth. She should have access to a secluded but familiar place, a whelping box generally made of wood, with dimensions that vary according to the size of the dog, but for a large-sized dog, it is about 120 x 180 cm, with sides of 40-50 cm. Inside, a balustrade can also be placed at about 20 cm high to prevent the mother from crushing the puppies. On the bottom, carpeting can be nailed down, which should be changed frequently. During winter, if the environment is not heated, it is advisable to place an infrared lamp over the box, taking care not to overheat it. During delivery, the female should be left as calm as possible, and generally, she does everything on her own without human intervention, but it is better to keep her under control.

MONITORING MATING

Carefully monitor mating to ensure that it occurs safely and that the dogs do not injure themselves. Generally, the male is brought by the female during the period when she allows him to cover her. The best time can be indicated not only by laboratory tests but also by observing the behavior of the female, who, when accepting the male, moves her tail to the side, especially if she is touched on the back. Some females are calm even in the presence of unknown males, while others are more nervous and need adequate time. The preliminary phase is characterized by courtship and ritual games. The two dogs sniff and lick each other until the female allows the male to mount her (mounting), allowing union (copulation). In some cases, the female does not accept the male and rejects him energetically and aggressively. This often depends on the wrong choice of period, but sometimes it can be related to the abnormal behavior of the female. In young subjects, it may happen that the male needs help and the female needs to be restrained, although it is always better for the two dogs to have all the time necessary for natural mating. During the mating, the penis erects and penetrates the vagina; shortly after, the male removes himself, and due to an anatomical peculiarity, he turns without being able to detach. The penis is flexed by about 180°, and the two dogs remain tail-to-tail, in this position, for an average time of 15-20 minutes, but it can vary from 5 to 45 minutes. During this second phase, prostatic fluid is ejaculated. Subsequently, the volume of the penis decreases, and the two subjects detach. It is important not to cause a violent detachment during this phase, as injuries to the genital organs could occur. Therefore, two people should assist in mating and be ready to hold the two subjects to prevent too abrupt a separation. It is advisable to carry out two or three matings, 24-48 hours apart.

Some mistakenly argue that if a female is mated several times in a short period, fertilized eggs can occur at different times, resulting in the birth of some full-term and others premature puppies. This is a belief that has no biological basis as ovulation is triggered by precise hormonal stimuli and occurs over a very short period. In wild canids, it is normal for mating to occur repeatedly as long as the female accepts the male, and there is no reason why this should harm the normal pregnancy of our dogs. Therefore, by repeating mating several times, 24-48 hours apart, we increase the probability of fertilization.

In cases where the two dogs cannot be mated naturally, artificial insemination can be used.

PREGNANCY

Taking care of the pregnant female: after mating, take care of the pregnant female and ensure she has a balanced diet and adequate veterinary care. Dealing with pregnancy, childbirth, and especially raising and weaning puppies can be an exciting and enjoyable experience, but it also requires sacrifice, especially time and a suitable place. Therefore, a pregnancy diagnosis is necessary, which is performed between the 20th and 25th day after mating, through abdominal palpation. The probability of error is high and depends on the size of the animal, its weight status, and the palpability of the abdomen.

After 20-25 days from mating, embryonic formations and fetal heartbeats can be detected with ultrasound examination. After 46-50 days from mating, the fetal ossification centers can be seen with radiographic examination.

The gestation period lasts an average of 60 to 63 days, with considerable variations, as the moment of fertilization of the eggs is not known, since the sperm can remain alive and vital in the female's body for a rather long time. Cases have been found where the pregnancy period varied between 57 and 72 days from mating. It is good practice to always record the dates of each mating. Regarding hormonal variations, the most constant data is the period that elapses between the LH (luteinizing hormone) peak, which is found about two days before ovulation, and delivery; this period lasts 64-66 days. In dogs, the fertilization of the egg does not occur immediately after ovulation, but the oocyte requires a maturation period of 2-3 days. During the first month of pregnancy, the female does not show any particular signs, only in the second month, a progressive abdominal enlargement is evident.

The pregnant female dog needs good physical exercise with at least one daily walk; however, excessive exertion and jumping should be avoided. During the second month, the diet should be improved, and meals brought to two, avoiding weight gain. A week before the expected event, the whelping box should be prepared in a secluded and quiet place.

THE BIRTH

1-2 weeks before the breasts swell and milk secretion may already begin, which can also be delayed until the day before birth. 2-3 days before, the female is calmer, tends to isolate herself, and eats less. The day before, she does not eat, and in the 12-24 hours prior, the rectal temperature drops by one degree Celsius. The pelvic and abdominal muscles relax. The female drinks but does not eat. It is therefore good to measure the temperature for a few days, always at the same time and record the data.

As the due date approaches, the female is generally restless, digs frantically, chews and destroys blankets or other materials and tries to create a "nest" in which to give birth. Breathing becomes more frequent.

Puppies usually present head-first with their front limbs extended forward, although a breech position is often encountered without complications for the birth. If one or two limbs and the head appear separately, the birth will be difficult. It is absolutely not necessary to pull as the tissues are still delicate and could be injured. It is sufficient to gently follow the pushes that the mother makes at regular intervals. The female, especially at her first delivery and if she is over three years old, may have some difficulty delivering the first puppy and may take up to an hour.

Each puppy is wrapped in a transparent sac (amniotic sac) which the female breaks immediately after birth (but it can also break during birth) and ingests. The puppy is then stimulated to breathe by the mother, who licks it intensely after breaking the umbilical cord with her teeth, chewing it insistently at the level of the abdomen. She then decisively pushes the puppy towards the nearest nipples. The placenta may be expelled attached to the umbilical cord or after 5-10 minutes from the birth of the individual puppy, and the mother takes care of eating it.

Usually, 2-3 hours pass between one puppy and the next, especially between the first and the second, and then the interval normally decreases. If the female is stressed, the last puppy may come out even after 18 hours.

The duration of delivery varies, depending on the number of puppies and other maternal factors, from 4 to 8 hours, and can last up to 24 hours. In any case, if more than eight hours have passed, it is advisable to consult a veterinarian.

During delivery, there are abundant dark green losses with reddish traces; they have an intense but not putrid odor. If they should appear yellowish, purulent, or malodorous, it could be a uterine infection with a serious danger to the mother and the puppies. The same greenish losses can also precede the birth of the first puppy by a few hours and are due to the emission of stagnant blood, produced by marginal hematomas, resulting from the detachment of the placenta. In case of difficulty, it is possible to resort to a cesarean section, which the veterinarian performs under general anesthesia. Twenty-four hours after delivery, have the female checked, especially in case of a temperature rise.

It is also important to verify that the uterus undergoes a normal involution process. In the following days, in fact, the uterus contracts, expelling membranes and clots; if the phenomenon is prolonged, has excessive intensity, or there is a putrefaction odor, consult a veterinarian. A few days later, due to the high number of puppies delivered, a form of tetany caused by calcium deficiency may appear, which is accumulated in the milk produced (eclampsia).

After giving birth, the female dog stays in the den for a long time and it is not easy to remove her. It is necessary to be careful because she can be particularly aggressive towards strangers and other dogs: her instinct drives her to defend her offspring. The nursing period lasts about 40-50 days until weaning, but already from the 20th-25th day, the puppies can be helped with artificial feeding. During lactation, it is necessary to check that the nipples are not sore and that all puppies are getting enough milk.

TAKING CARE OF THE PUPPIES

Once the puppies are born, take care of them and ensure that they have a clean and safe environment. Provide them with the right nutrition and medical assistance. It is also necessary to plan in advance who, or through which channels, to give away the weaned puppies.

FALSE PREGNANCY

This condition is quite common and also occurs in normal female dogs. The symptoms appear two months after the last heat and resemble those of a normal pregnant dog: hunger, thirst, sometimes vomiting, restlessness, and in some cases abdominal swelling. Lactation appears in the last period and causes serious problems of mastitis since there are no puppies to suckle the milk. The cause of this pathology seems to be the level of blood progesterone.

UNDESIRED MATING

There is a theory that undesired mating can affect future litters. This theory, called "telegony," was supported at the beginning of the last century but is now totally rejected based on current biological knowledge. According to this theory, a dog that, unfortunately, had been "seduced" by a mixed breed would suffer negative consequences even in subsequent litters.

There is no reason to worry: every pregnancy and its respective litters are influenced solely and exclusively by the parents of that precise mating. Unfortunately, there are still some who believe in "telegony."

The Labrador reproduction process and the journey to parenthood are ways to deepen your understanding of this wonderful breed and appreciate the beauty and complexity of the life cycle. Whether you are a breeder or a Labrador enthusiast, this section of the book will provide you with the necessary information to understand and appreciate the reproduction process and the joy of Labrador parenthood.

A Comprehensive Guide to Care, Communication, and Adventures with Your Loyal Companion

CHAPTER 8 - CHOOSING THE PERFECT LABRADOR: FINDING YOUR IDEAL COMPANION

Choosing the right dog is a crucial step in ensuring a deep and lasting connection with your pet. This chapter will provide you with detailed information on various aspects to consider when selecting a Labrador, including gender, age, temperament, and origin of the dog. By following these guidelines, you will be able to make an informed decision and find your ideal companion.

Are you looking for a family companion, a working dog, or a companion for physical activity? Identify your specific needs to help you make a targeted decision.

Labradors are energetic dogs that require regular exercise. Evaluate whether you are capable of meeting their physical activity and mental engagement needs.

Differences between males and females: Male Labradors tend to be slightly larger than females and may exhibit a more dominant temperament. Females can be more affectionate and territorial. Consider these differences and decide which best fits your preferences and home environment.

Puppy or adult: Puppies require constant attention and training, while an adult dog may already be trained and have an established temperament. Assess your willingness to handle the growth phase and initial training of a puppy or if you prefer a more mature dog.

Temperament and character: Spend time with the Labrador you are considering to assess its temperament and personality. Observe its energy level, responsiveness, sociability, and affinity with you and your family members.

Seek input from the breeder or shelter staff to gather information about the dogs' temperaments and their suitability for different family situations.

Consider whether you desire a purebred dog and are willing to seek a reputable breeder or if you prefer to adopt a Labrador from a shelter. Both options can provide wonderful dogs, but ensure you conduct thorough research and ask questions about the dog's background.

Educate yourself about recommended genetic tests and health certifications for Labrador Retrievers, such as testing for hip and elbow dysplasia. Make sure the dog you are considering has passed such tests and received a good health evaluation.

Gather information about the breeder or shelter, such as their reputation, the quality of care provided to the dogs, and the support they offer after adoption.

A Comprehensive Guide to Care, Communication, and Adventures with Your Loyal Companion

> Schedule visits to meet the breeder or visit the shelter and observe the conditions in which the dogs are kept. Ask any necessary questions to ensure the Labrador comes from a reliable source and has been well-cared for.

Before deciding to purchase a Labrador, you should ask yourself some fundamental questions:

Firstly, do you know the characteristics and needs of a dog of this size and with this particular temperament?

It is important to choose a breed not just because it is trendy or based on hearsay, but because you are genuinely convinced that it is the right dog for you.

Secondly, are you willing to sacrifice a good part of your time to devote yourself to your new friend?

The Labrador is a docile and patient dog that easily adapts to any situation, but it needs to be with its owner and taken outdoors to give vent to its natural vitality. This is a commitment that, being undoubtedly greater than that of a puppy, remains the same throughout the life of your companion.

Thirdly, but no less important, are the people around you in contrast to your choice?

Is everyone in your family in favor of adopting a puppy? There is nothing worse, for you and the dog, than living in a forced compromise situation with your neighbors, the doorman, or even worse, with your family members.

Once you have completed this "examination of conscience," you will undoubtedly be ready to welcome the little Labrador.

Where to buy it? Since it is an animal that will become our companion for several years, it is important not to buy "blindly." For this reason, the best thing to do is to contact one or more breeders and ask for an appointment.

Whether you want a good hunting dog, a show dog, or simply a faithful companion, the breeder will be the one who can best advise you in your choice.

THE VISIT TO THE BREEDING FARM

If the breeding farm you have chosen is not too far away, you can make a first visit even when the puppies are still small. On this occasion, you will not choose your dog yet, but you can see the parents (at least the mother and sometimes also the father) or other subjects of the same origin, check the hygiene conditions and the type of breeding: generally, the true breeder, serious and passionate, selects only one breed, or in any case few. It is important that the puppies are raised in close contact with humans in order to receive the necessary imprinting; a good breeder generally does not deliver the puppies until two months, two and a half months after birth. During your visit, the most important thing will be to establish a relationship of mutual trust with the person who will sell you the dog and who can offer you all the necessary advice for any problems of feeding, education, training, reproduction, and so on through. You will have the opportunity to get to know him, but above all to make yourself known, so that he himself can advise you on the most congenial dog for you. If you have a family with young children, he will choose the quietest and least boisterous puppy for you; if you are an enthusiastic hunter, he will advise you on the most enterprising and lively one; if in the future you want your dog to reproduce, he will advise you on the most suitable female, etc. When the fateful day finally arrives, once in front of the litter, you will realize that the choice is not easy at all. All the puppies will seem so adorable to you that you will find yourself in serious difficulty. It will therefore be the breeder, who knows every puppy and, to your surprise, can distinguish it perhaps among eight others, to illustrate the strengths and weaknesses of each one. In any case, you can also try to make the choice: if you have decided on a female, do not look at the males, focus only on the females; you can have all the puppies of the same sex put together and observe them as they play with each other, you can ask to pick them up, to follow you, to see them standing still and in an exhibition position, to check their teeth and fur. Bear in mind that not all breeders like strangers to touch the puppies, however, it is very important to establish a physical contact with the dog because many times the choice is made instinctively without particular observations or reasoning. A healthy puppy must be lively, not shy away or give up playing, must have a beautiful thick coat, a lively look and clear eyes without excessive tearing or mucus accumulated around the eyes. Size is not particularly important; even in a very homogeneous litter, there may be variations of one or two kilograms of weight at the age of two months without necessarily influencing future development. However, it is best to avoid buying the smallest puppy if the size difference from its siblings is excessive, in which case it is likely that it had problems growing. It is a common belief that the biggest puppy is also the most beautiful: this is not always true; too rapid or excessive growth compared to the average can, in some cases, lead to oversized, "exaggerated" subjects. Morphologically, the small Labrador must be compact, with sturdy-boned limbs and well-developed feet. The chest must be deep, the head square with not overly large ears. The eyes sometimes do not yet have the definitive color, but in a two-month-old puppy, they should already be dark enough.

Regarding the temperament, it is very important that the Labrador puppy is not shy and does not growl or try to bite you when you reach out to pet it. On the contrary, a good Labrador puppy should come towards you wagging its tail and not resist if you pick it up. The retriever instinct can be evident from a young age, as the little Labrador loves to carry objects of all kinds from one place to another and is often seen with toys, bones, etc. in its mouth.

WHEN TO ACQUIRE IT

The best age to bring home your puppy is between two months and two and a half months old. At this time, the puppies are completely weaned and have already started their basic vaccination program. Moreover, from a canine psychology point of view, this phase corresponds to the imprinting period, when the puppy gets to know the world and becomes accustomed to different situations. If a puppy is brought to its new home too late, there is a risk that it will not adapt easily. However, this can happen if the puppy has not been accustomed to close contact with humans during breeding. Typically, the breeder takes care to accustom the puppies to various situations they will encounter in the

A Comprehensive Guide to Care, Communication, and Adventures with Your Loyal Companion

future, in order to make them balanced in character.

MALE OR FEMALE

The choice of the sex of a Labrador Retriever puppy depends mainly on the owner's personal preferences and the characteristics of the animal. Generally, males should be livelier and more impetuous and, having a more massive constitution, they require a firmer hand from their owner more frequently. Females, on the other hand, are generally more gentle and calm, tend to be a bit lighter and more agile than males. However, it should be kept in mind that there are exceptions: a female with an outgoing temperament can be much livelier than a large, docile, and cuddly male.

If you do not have the possibility to control your dog in the place where it lives, it is better to buy a male, as this will prevent unwanted mating during the heat period. If your garden is "unassailable" by male suitors who will inevitably court your female dog, a female can be just fine, as long as you pay attention to prevent her from running away. If you have neighbors with other dogs, keep in mind that the Labrador usually has a good temperament and likes to play with its peers. The male can become quarrelsome with dogs of the same sex in the presence of females or due to territorial instinct, but this is still a relatively rare event.

Regarding work, there are no big differences in ability between males and females. However, the female must absolutely be left at home during the heat period. Therefore, if you want to continue your hunting activity, you will definitely have to choose a male. The same goes for the show career: a female in heat may not have problems in the ring, but it can cause disturbance if introduced to a show, and it is also prohibited by the regulations.

In general, the personality and behavior of the dog depend heavily on training and socialization, regardless of sex. Therefore, it is important to choose a puppy that fits your lifestyle and needs, rather than basing your decision solely on sex. In any case, it is important to acquire a puppy from a reliable and responsible breeder who takes care of the welfare of the animals and guarantees that the puppy is healthy and socialized.

BLACK, YELLOW OR CHOCOLATE

A Comprehensive Guide to Care, Communication, and Adventures with Your Loyal Companion

The choice of coat color for a Labrador Retriever depends mainly on the personal preferences of the owner, as the color of the coat does not affect the dog's personality or behavior, and also on the availability of the breeder. Sometimes, it is not possible to find a puppy of the desired gender and color. As previously mentioned, Labrador Retrievers can have a black, yellow, or chocolate coat, which are the standard colors recognized by most kennel clubs. Some Labrador Retrievers may also have a silver or champagne coat, but these are not considered standard colors. Apart from the rather rare and sought-after chocolate color, the other two colors, which are certainly more common, are both very beautiful. The black coat is less recommended for those who live in regions with a hot climate, as black attracts the sun's rays more than yellow. A Labrador with a shiny black coat is certainly one of the most beautiful animals to see, but it is also true that a black dog, as with other breeds, must have a perfect profile to be truly appreciated. As for yellow, it can be more or less intense; coats that are too white or excessively reddish should be considered negative. It is not a dirtier coat than black, and being a recessive trait, it has been selectively bred by breeders. Yellow-coated dogs more frequently have less pronounced pigmentation of the nose, which, instead of being black, can be brown. It is important to note that coat color should never be the determining factor in choosing a puppy. It is much more important to choose a puppy from a reliable and responsible breeder who cares for the animals' welfare and ensures that the puppy is healthy and socialized. Additionally, it is important to choose a puppy that fits your lifestyle and needs, regardless of coat color.

Choosing the perfect Labrador Retriever requires time, reflection, and thorough research. Carefully consider your needs, lifestyle, and key factors such as gender, age, temperament, and the dog's origin. Consult reputable breeders and local shelters, seek advice, and gather information on the dog's health and post-adoption support. With careful planning and attention to detail, you will be able to find your ideal companion, a Labrador that will bring joy, love, and companionship into your life.

A Comprehensive Guide to Care, Communication, and Adventures with Your Loyal Companion

CHAPTER 9 - BREEDING A PUPPY

Breeding a Labrador puppy is definitely a unique experience. It does require time and commitment, but it is very rewarding. Breeding a dog includes:

- Feeding the puppy
- Health
- Legal obligations
- First day with the puppy

• Physical activity You will realize how many things you can do with your dog and how many times it will be able to satisfy you, especially from an emotional point of view. From the moment the puppy enters your home, especially if you have never owned a dog before, your life will be a bit "revolutionized", but at the same time it will acquire new, interesting and stimulating aspects. The emotional side will be the most important, as acquiring a puppy means acquiring a new member of the family.

PUPPY FEEDING

Pic-15 by Chathura Anuradha Subasinghe on Unsplash

At the time of purchase, the breeder will indicate what food the puppy is accustomed to and what times it should eat.

The puppy requires a complete and balanced diet without vitamin and mineral deficiencies but also without excesses. Depending on your availability of time and your preference, you can choose either homemade food, which has the advantage of being more controllable in terms of ingredients, although more difficult to balance, or ready-made industrial puppy food, which is undoubtedly more convenient, more balanced, but less "genuine."

Labrador puppies are generally very greedy, so be careful to avoid overfeeding. Rarely will a puppy become overweight if overfed, but it will tend to grow much faster and become excessively heavy for its skeletal system, which is still forming and consolidating. It is much better for a six-month-old puppy to be slightly smaller and lighter than average rather than too big.

Do not be afraid that if not fed enough, the puppy will not become a normal-sized adult. It will simply take longer to get there but will be less at risk of developing bone or joint problems typical of rapidly growing breeds.

Unfortunately, the current trend, also driven by pet food manufacturers, is to give too much rather than too little to eat, and this has negative repercussions on the harmonious growth of puppies.

During growth, it is a good idea to monitor the puppy's weight. The breeder will have already done so daily for the first month of life and then two or three times a week during the second month. After two months, you can weigh it every two weeks and note any changes. Typically, puppies grow at a rate of 700 grams per kilogram each week, so avoid exceeding this growth rate. Present the puppy with its bowl and leave it for twenty minutes or half an hour at most. If it has not finished its ration after this time, remove the bowl. It is better to get the puppy used to eating at specific times rather than having food available all the time.

If you have had the puppies at home since the first day of birth, it is advisable to start integrating maternal feeding with some meals consisting of milk and one egg yolk per 100 ml around the 25th day of age. After the 30th day, the weaning process begins with a drier diet. Early weaning saves the mother and is very useful in large litters. The puppies are separated from the mother for progressively longer periods, and between 45 and 55 days, they must be weaned and fed only artificially. At the beginning of weaning, some finely ground or pureed meat is added to the cow's milk, which can also be replaced with baby food. Then a drier diet consisting of good quality meat and/or fish, well-cooked rice and/or cereal flakes, milk, a little oil, vitamins, and minerals is introduced.

Milk, meat, and fish should be predominant over cereals, constituting 80% of the ration at 40 days and 60% at 60. Gradually, the amount of cereal is increased relative to the meat. The meat can be served raw if of good quality, but it is better to cook it.

One meal a day can consist of biscuit bread and milk. Throughout the growth period, a raw egg yolk can be offered three or four times a week, and cheese can be used partially as a substitute for meat. The vitamin-mineral supplement should have adequate levels of calcium and phosphorus.

HEALTH

You must ensure first and foremost that the breeder provides you with the health booklet where the dates of deworming and first vaccinations performed will be recorded, as well as the dates on which the vaccinations themselves will need to be recalled at your expense. It is necessary to follow the change of teeth from milk teeth to permanent teeth because in some cases there can be double dentition (especially in canines) that hinders chewing. The transition from milk teeth to permanent teeth begins at three and a half months and ends at six months, when even the permanent canines have reached their maximum length. If they do not fall out spontaneously, the milk teeth will need to be removed by the veterinarian. In any case, it is important for the puppy to get used to leaving its mouth open and to have its teeth and tongue touched for occasional checks.

LEGAL OBLIGATIONS

Dog registration: in many countries, there is a canine registry that tracks information about owners, dogs, and vaccinations. In some countries, dog registration is mandatory. Microchipping: in many countries, dogs must be microchipped to ensure identification. The microchip is a subcutaneous device that contains a unique code that allows for the identification of the dog and its owner. Vaccinations: most countries require that dogs be vaccinated against some diseases such as rabies and parvovirus for all dogs over three months old. Leash and muzzle: in many countries, dogs must

A Comprehensive Guide to Care, Communication, and Adventures with Your Loyal Companion

be kept on a leash and with a muzzle when in public places. Education and care of the dog: dog owners are required to properly educate and care for their animals, in order to ensure their well-being and safety. This includes training the dog, caring for its hygiene and health, and preventing dangerous behaviors. These are just some of the main legal obligations that may apply to the purchase or adoption of a puppy, but it is important to check local laws to ensure that all regulations in force in your area are being respected. The identification data of the puppy, including the microchip number, must be clearly recorded in the booklet next to the vaccination vouchers, and the signature and stamp of the veterinarian who performed them. The puppy must already have been equipped with a microchip as, according to a recent rule, unregistered puppies cannot be registered in the pedigree book. The name of the dog may have already been chosen by the breeder, who usually names the litter with the same initial; in some cases, you will be allowed to name the dog of your choice, always following the initial rule. For puppies purchased from private individuals, it will be easier to choose the name.

FIRST DAY WITH YOUR PUPPY

On the day you go to pick up your puppy, you should first notify the breeder so that they can fast before the car ride. In any case, make sure to have tissues, newspapers or rags with you, in case the puppy gets car sick. Bring a bottle of fresh water and a bowl for them to drink from if it gets hot. Don't go alone, it's better to have someone drive so that you can take care of the puppy. Keep in mind that it's much better for the puppy to travel in your arms rather than bouncing around in the trunk of the car. It's their first time alone, without their siblings, in a new environment, and your presence will definitely reassure them. Once they've calmed down or even fallen asleep, you can put them at your feet, on the mat in front of the seat. Don't be afraid to spoil them by holding them during their first trip: when they are older and know what traveling in a car means, you can put them wherever you want. During the trip, especially if it lasts more than two hours, make stops to allow the puppy to relieve themselves, but be careful not to leave them in places where other dogs may have been. Such a young puppy is not yet protected against infectious diseases since they have not completed their basic vaccination program, so they risk contracting some disease if they come into contact with environmental viruses. Also, if you don't have a leash to keep them, be very careful not to let them run away. Don't leave them alone in the car when you stop, especially if it's hot, and make sure to always keep the window slightly open. If there are curves or bends, always drive very slowly to avoid making them sick. Puppies, like children, are very sensitive to motion sickness. As an adult, they usually stay calm in the car and are not one of those dogs that tend to jump from one seat to another barking like crazy. You just need a little patience to teach them where to stay and to teach them to only get out when asked to. After that, you can tackle even long trips without any problem. When traveling, always get used to bringing a bowl and fresh water with you. In the car, the dog can stay on a blanket; if you have a station wagon, you can get them used to staying in the rear compartment used as a trunk, while if you

A Comprehensive Guide to Care, Communication, and Adventures with Your Loyal Companion

have a sedan, you will have to teach them to stay at the foot of the seat. The Highway Code prohibits transporting animals without an approved protective net for the driver, so at least avoid letting the dog sit in the front seat as there may be penalties. Very useful, especially if you have more than one dog, are travel crates: these are wooden or metal cages that can be placed in the trunk of family cars. If the animals are in cages, they are less likely to be harmed in the event of an accident or sudden braking.

PHYSICAL ACTIVITY

Labradors are active dogs and require regular exercise to maintain good health and mental balance. Plan interactive play sessions, walks, retrieval games, and other activities that suit your dog's needs. In addition to physical exercise, provide your Labrador with mental stimulation activities such as intelligence games, hide-and-seek games, or the use of interactive toys to keep them mentally engaged and satisfied.

To achieve proper psychophysical development, your puppy should dedicate several hours a day to play. However, this playtime, at least during the first six months, must be necessarily controlled. All excessively violent games, perhaps with other dogs, wild runs in the fields, "up and down" the stairs, etc., should be avoided. You can get your puppy used to playing with you by throwing objects at a short distance for him to retrieve or simulating still fights with him, but it is very important that until the ossification is complete, all types of effort that excessively stress the skeleton and joints should be avoided. The puppy should, therefore, be kept at rest until six months of age. Walks must be strictly on a leash to prevent him from running wild with other dogs. Physical exercise is necessary, but it must always be moderate; the muscles must be developed, but this must not happen at the expense of other equally important organs for locomotion. Once the puppy turns one year old, a more intense training program will begin to favor muscle development. You can take your dog for a run with you, perhaps using a bike; you should also make him swim as often as possible to develop the pectoral muscles. It is important to dedicate yourself to playing with the puppy at least two or three times a day. In this way, he will begin to distinguish the moments in which he must be calm from those in which he can have fun; furthermore, by doing so, he will get tired enough and avoid causing trouble when left alone. Lastly, if set up correctly, playtime can be the basis for a dog's future training.

A Comprehensive Guide to Care, Communication, and Adventures with Your Loyal Companion

CHAPTER 10 - CARING FOR YOUR LABRADOR: NURTURING A HEALTHY AND HAPPY PET

This crucial chapter focuses on the importance of taking complete and loving care of your Labrador Retriever. From maintaining a balanced diet to caring for exercise needs, hygiene, and health, providing proper care for your Labrador is essential to ensure that your dog is healthy, happy, and well-balanced.

This chapter will guide you through the essential aspects of caring for your Labrador, providing practical tips and useful information to create an optimal care environment for your four-legged friend.

The Labrador is a hardy breed that requires few special care needs. Once a balanced diet and sufficient exercise are ensured, everything else boils down to some attention to the more delicate organs.

COAT

Regularly brush your Labrador's coat to remove dead hair and prevent matting. Labrador coats require special care, especially during shedding seasons.

Even yellow individuals have the extraordinary ability to stay naturally clean, perhaps aided by the frequent baths our friend loves to take. Its texture allows it to eliminate any type of dirt or mud within a few hours.

To keep it well-groomed, a bath from time to time is necessary, but as infrequently as possible. A good rule is to get the dog used to a daily brushing to remove dead hair: in this way, you will avoid, at least in part, finding stray hairs around the house. If the dog gets wet, you can dry it with a sponge towel or a chamois leather.

When brushing, avoid brushes with steel teeth or de-shedding tools that tend to pull and thin out the undercoat. You can use a natural bristle brush for this purpose and run it over the dog's coat following the direction of the hair.

Lastly, you can run a woolen cloth over the hair to make it shinier.

The Labrador should never be shaved, not even in the summer. In fact, the dense coat, with its impenetrable undercoat, represents an insulating layer even against the heat. The only time it is allowed to use scissors is to slightly shorten the hair on the tails of show dogs.

The Labrador's coat undergoes a natural shedding process. There are periods, called molts, in which there is abundant shedding of the undercoat. The molt usually occurs with the arrival of warm weather, in outdoor dogs; in "indoor" dogs, this cycle can be altered by winter heating.

TEETH

Regularly brush your Labrador's teeth to remove food residue, prevent cavities, or other oral cavity infections like tartar, especially after 18 months of age.

Teeth should be periodically checked for cleanliness. As for tooth cleaning, there are currently dog

A Comprehensive Guide to Care, Communication, and Adventures with Your Loyal Companion

toothpaste and toothbrushes available on the market.

However, if the food is not too soft, it is not necessary to intervene every day; once a week is sufficient.

A frequent problem, which occurs mainly in older dogs, is the formation of tartar, which, if excessive, can cause gingivitis with bad breath and, in more severe cases, tooth loss. In these cases, the veterinarian must intervene to remove the tartar.

EYES

Eyes do not need any special care; it is sufficient to clean them with a cotton ball soaked in boric acid solution at the corners, where a bit of mucus sometimes accumulates. They should be checked by a veterinarian if excessive tearing or redness of the conjunctiva occurs.

EAR CARE

Gently clean your Labrador's ears to prevent the buildup of wax and prevent ear infections.

The ears represent a particular problem as Labradors have droopy ears and, especially as water-loving dogs, are prone to ear infections. Ear care consists of periodic cleaning using specific products that dissolve earwax. It is better to avoid using cotton-tipped swabs as they can push the dirt deeper into the ear canal.

If an ear product is applied, it is enough to make the dog shake its head to remove the contents from the ear canal. If you notice that your dog frequently shakes its head, scratches its ears, and emits an unpleasant odor, it is best to have it examined by a veterinarian.

NAIL

Keep your Labrador's nails trimmed to prevent them from becoming too long and causing discomfort or walking issues. Nails, especially those of the front legs that tend to wear less, should be periodically trimmed. To do this, you need nail clippers made specifically for dogs; the first time, you can ask the veterinarian to show you how to do it, or else you risk cutting too much and making the live part of the nail bleed. With experience, you can do it easily on your own. If you make a mistake, stop the bleeding with a normal hemostatic product and disinfect the bleeding nail.

Trimming the nails of your Labrador is an important part of general care. Overgrown nails can cause discomfort for the dog during walking and may also be prone to breakage or slipping. Here are some tips for trimming your Labrador's nails:

- Purchase nail clippers specifically designed for large dogs. Avoid using scissors or human nail clippers as they may damage the dog's nails.

- Get your Labrador accustomed to paw handling from a young age. Regularly pet and touch their paws so that they become comfortable with the contact.

- Carefully observe your dog's nails and identify the point where the transparent part ends and the darker, thicker part begins. This transparent area is called the "quick" and contains blood vessels and nerves. You should avoid cutting into the quick to prevent bleeding and discomfort for the dog.

- Start by trimming a small portion of the nail at a time, being careful not to get too close to the quick.

A Comprehensive Guide to Care, Communication, and Adventures with Your Loyal Companion

If your dog has light-colored nails, it may be easier to identify the quick. If they have dark nails, you may need to proceed with extra caution and trim a little at a time.

- If you accidentally cut into the quick and the dog starts bleeding, apply cotton or a styptic powder to stop the bleeding. If the bleeding doesn't stop or if you have any concerns, consult your veterinarian.

- After each nail trimming session, reward your Labrador with affection or a small treat to positively associate the experience.

- If you don't feel confident in trimming your dog's nails on your own, you can seek help from your veterinarian or a professional groomer. Make sure to trim the nails regularly, typically every 4-6 weeks, to maintain the comfort and health of your Labrador's paws.

- Keep your Labrador's nails trimmed to prevent them from becoming too long and causing discomfort or walking issues

CHAPTER 11 - FEEDING YOUR LABRADOR: A BALANCED DIET FOR OPTIMAL HEALTH

Proper nutrition is essential for the well-being and health of your Labrador. In this chapter, we will explore the importance of a balanced diet, key nutrients your dog needs, and some guidelines to ensure your Labrador receives the right nutritional intake.

Labradors are active, medium to large-sized dogs that require a balanced diet to meet their energy and nutritional needs.

A balanced diet should include high-quality proteins, carbohydrates, healthy fats, vitamins, and minerals.

Proteins: Proteins are essential for muscle health and maintaining a strong immune system. Good sources of high-quality proteins for your Labrador include lean meats like chicken, turkey, beef, and fish.

Carbohydrates: Carbohydrates provide energy for your Labrador. Opt for complex carbohydrates like whole grains, brown rice, and sweet potatoes, which offer sustained energy.

Healthy fats: Fats are important for skin and coat health, as well as proper nervous system function. Make sure your Labrador's diet includes healthy fats like fish oil, coconut oil, and vegetable oils.

Vitamins and minerals: Vitamins and minerals are crucial for optimal health. Ensure your Labrador receives a variety of fresh fruits and vegetables to provide an adequate intake of vitamins and minerals.

It is important to maintain your Labrador's weight under control to avoid health issues related to obesity. Follow the feeding guidelines recommended by your veterinarian and be mindful of portion sizes to prevent overfeeding.

Some Labradors may have specific dietary needs, such as allergies or food intolerances. If you have any doubts or experience health issues related to diet, always consult your veterinarian for a thorough evaluation.

If you need to make changes to your Labrador's diet, do so gradually to avoid digestive upset. Introduce new foods slowly, mixing them with your dog's regular food over several days.

Ensure your Labrador always has access to a source of fresh and clean water. Water is essential for hydration and proper bodily function.

Observe your Labrador closely for any signs of food intolerances, allergies, or general health changes. If you notice anything unusual, contact your veterinarian for guidance.

Choose a high-quality diet specifically formulated to meet the nutritional needs of Labrador Retrievers, taking into account their age, weight, and activity level.

Establish a regular feeding routine, dividing meals into appropriate portions and providing them according to your veterinarian's recommendations. Proper nutrition is essential for the well-being and health of your Labrador. In this chapter, we will

A Comprehensive Guide to Care, Communication, and Adventures with Your Loyal Companion

explore the importance of a balanced diet, key nutrients your dog needs, and some guidelines to ensure your Labrador receives the right nutritional intake.

Labradors are active, medium to large-sized dogs that require a balanced diet to meet their energy and nutritional needs.

A balanced diet should include high-quality proteins, carbohydrates, healthy fats, vitamins, and minerals.

Proteins: Proteins are essential for muscle health and maintaining a strong immune system. Good sources of high-quality proteins for your Labrador include lean meats like chicken, turkey, beef, and fish.

Carbohydrates: Carbohydrates provide energy for your Labrador. Opt for complex carbohydrates like whole grains, brown rice, and sweet potatoes, which offer sustained energy.

Healthy fats: Fats are important for skin and coat health, as well as proper nervous system function. Make sure your Labrador's diet includes healthy fats like fish oil, coconut oil, and vegetable oils.

Vitamins and minerals: Vitamins and minerals are crucial for optimal health. Ensure your Labrador receives a variety of fresh fruits and vegetables to provide an adequate intake of vitamins and minerals.

It is important to maintain your Labrador's weight under control to avoid health issues related to obesity. Follow the feeding guidelines recommended by your veterinarian and be mindful of portion sizes to prevent overfeeding.

Some Labradors may have specific dietary needs, such as allergies or food intolerances. If you have any doubts or experience health issues related to diet, always consult your veterinarian for a thorough evaluation.

If you need to make changes to your Labrador's diet, do so gradually to avoid digestive upset. Introduce new foods slowly, mixing them with your dog's regular food over several days.

Ensure your Labrador always has access to a source of fresh and clean water. Water is essential for hydration and proper bodily function.

Observe your Labrador closely for any signs of food intolerances, allergies, or general health changes. If you notice anything unusual, contact your veterinarian for guidance.

Choose a high-quality diet specifically formulated to meet the nutritional needs of Labrador Retrievers, taking into account their age, weight, and activity level.

Establish a regular feeding routine, dividing meals into appropriate portions and providing them according to your veterinarian's recommendations.

Like all animals, dogs also need a constant supply of nutrients and to be fed properly. Dogs have limited chewing ability and swallow food very quickly. Food, especially solid food, remains in the stomach for a long time (3-12 hours) and is transformed into a slurry before passing into the intestine where assimilation occurs. Nutrients are transported through the blood to various tissues that need to be nourished. Due to the characteristics of the canine digestive system, dogs can consume large meals and have a prolonged interval between meals, as stomach emptying occurs slowly. Coarse, rather than finely ground food, is preferable.

Dogs are carnivorous animals, but a long process of adaptation and coexistence with humans has led them to also consume non-animal products. However, they still require a concentrated, high-nutrient diet that varies depending on the breed, age, physiological state (maintenance, growth, reproduction, lactation), and climate. To achieve the best results, we must feed our dogs in a way that provides them with adequate amounts of nutrients: proteins, carbohydrates, and fats, as well as vitamins and minerals. The diet must be well-balanced, meaning the various nutrients must be in the right proportions to avoid excess or deficiency. Optimal nutrition is essential to keep the dog in good health, not excessively fat or thin, and with a beautiful coat. This aspect is even more important during the puppy's growth phase, which requires particular attention and care. To feed our dogs well, it is necessary to know the biological meaning of the different nutrients and possible sources of intake.

Occasionally observe fat deposits on the withers, rump, and ribs to see if your dog is overweight. Weigh them regularly and record their weight. If they are overweight, strictly eliminate snacks and kitchen leftovers, and resist their pleading gaze. This is a bad habit due to the owner's too "kind heart" who occasionally gives them a treat. Never feed the dog when you sit at the table or during meal preparation. Make them eat before you and, if necessary, do not let them assist.

If necessary, feed them with special low-energy but well-balanced diets with the right level of protein and vitamin-mineral supplementation. Give them moist meals with the right amount of fiber. To distract them from hunger, leave them some fake bones to gnaw on. But above all, make sure there are no diseases due to hormonal and metabolic dysfunctions. And lastly, make them move more.

In general, you can choose a series of foods that can vary depending on seasonal needs or health status and a natural life diet that can include the following regime:

Leftovers from the kitchen must not violate the fundamental rules of nutrition.
Freshly seared beef, chicken, or turkey.
Very dry or toasted bread. A little olive oil.
Hot broth.
Vitamin and mineral supplement.
Frozen meat.
Well-cooked rice or pasta.
Mixed vegetables.
A little olive oil.
Vitamin and mineral supplement.
Frozen cereal flakes or puffed rice.
A tablespoon of bran.

Hot water (the supplement is generally already present).

Complete feed in kibble, extruded, or cube form (administer according to label instructions).

Complete feed in flakes to soak in hot water, broth, or milk (administer according to instructions).

ENERGY

Even during moments of rest, the body needs energy. Nutrients are transported to the various cells of the body where, in the presence of oxygen, they are transformed into energy. During this process of transformation, heat is also produced, allowing the dog to maintain its own temperature.

The more active an animal is, the higher the amount of food that needs to be transformed into energy. Puppies have almost triple the energy requirements compared to adults. The energy value of food is generally expressed in metabolizable energy (ME) and measured in kilocalories (Cal) or Mega Joules (MJ). Energy-dense fats provide an intake that is about double that of sugars and proteins.

Excess energy is usually stored by the body in the form of fat deposits. It is therefore useful to weigh our dogs regularly and record their weight to check for normal weight gain.

NUTRIENTS
CARBOHYDRATES OR GLUCIDES:

They are a source of energy necessary for muscle work and various activities of the body. Some have a simple structure (fructose, lactose, etc.), others like starch have a more complex structure. Both in adults and puppies, an excess of sucrose may not be well tolerated and can cause diarrhea due to the low presence of the specific enzyme (sucrase) in the dog's intestine; similarly, adult dogs may poorly digest milk due to a lack of lactase.

Among the dog's foods, starch is the most important carbohydrate and we find it abundant in cereals such as wheat (bread), corn (polenta, flakes, etc.), rice, etc. Starch must be well cooked or undergo other physical treatments to be digested by the dog.

Cellulose, hemicellulose, and crude fiber, generally contained in many vegetables, are not digested by dogs. Therefore, the higher their content, the lower the energy value. However, the presence of a little fiber in the diet, especially in elderly or sedentary individuals, can be useful to prevent them from gaining weight and to maintain regular intestinal functionality.

FATS OR LIPIDS:

They are essential to the body as they are components of cells. They provide energy and therefore heat to the body. Those present in the body as storage fats (subcutaneous, perivisceral, intramuscular) serve as an energy reserve that the body draws on when food intake is insufficient, and also act as a thermal insulator. Some lipid compounds play important roles as cellular constituents (phospholipids, glycolipids) and bioregulators (cholesterol, hormones, fat-soluble vitamins, bile acids). They are present in all foods, and we can distinguish between those of plant origin (oils) and those of animal origin (lard, fat, etc.). Their presence in the diet is indispensable.

PROTEINS:

They are plastic foods that contribute to the construction of the body and are necessary for the formation of new cells. They have an essential function in the formation, maintenance, and repair of muscles, bones, and organs. Protein requirements are particularly high in puppies and during growth. They can be of animal origin such as those in meat, milk, fish, and eggs, or of plant origin such as those in soy, peas, beans, etc. The biological value of proteins and their utilization depend on the ratio

A Comprehensive Guide to Care, Communication, and Adventures with Your Loyal Companion

of various amino acids. Since it is not possible to store amino acids, they must be provided with the daily protein diet.

MINERAL SALTS:

Depending on the amount present in the body, they are divided into macro-elements (calcium, phosphorus, sulfur, sodium, chlorine, potassium, magnesium) and micro-elements (iron, copper, zinc, manganese, iodine, selenium, cobalt, molybdenum). They are essential components of body tissues and have both plastic and bioregulatory functions, participating in many biochemical processes and performing vital functions such as maintaining the osmotic pressure and acid-base balance of body fluids, muscle contraction, nerve transmission, the formation of some enzymes and hormones. They participate in the formation of the skeleton and are therefore very important for growing animals. They are contained in bone meal, milk, cheese, fish, meat, and many vegetables. In a dog's diet, it is essential to supplement the diet with mineral salts, and it is important to maintain a correct ratio between some of them, such as calcium-phosphorus, iron-copper, etc.

VITAMINS: They are divided into fat-soluble (A, D, E, K) and water-soluble (B1, B2, pantothenic acid, nicotinic acid, B6, folic acid, H, B12, choline, C); they act in very small quantities, intervening in many essential organic processes. The deficiency of one or more vitamins can lead to serious imbalances and dysfunctions. However, excesses of some vitamins are harmful and can cause serious problems. They are generally produced by plant organisms and are found in the liver, eggs, cereal germs, yeast, vegetable and animal oils. They can be easily destroyed by light and heat, so they should always be added to warm, not boiling, feed. It is also important to note that ready-made foods often contain vitamins (declared on the label): their accumulation could lead to harmful excesses.

FOODS

MEAT:

It can be from beef, chicken, or other animals. Raw meat is better digested, but if it is not fresh and of good quality, it is preferable to boil it. In any case, it should be cooked lightly. Pork should always be cooked to avoid the risk of infections (Aujeszky's disease) and infestations (trichinosis). The protein and energy content varies depending on the percentage of bones and fat present. Digestibility and biological value are higher with a greater percentage of muscle content and decrease when there is a high presence of tendons, cartilage, and collagen in general. Dogs can also digest meat that is starting to putrefy thanks to the high amount of gastric juices they are able to produce.

OFFAL:

They are made up of organs such as the heart, liver, tripe, spleen, etc., generally very appetizing to dogs even though they have a lower protein content than muscle. They are excellent foods, especially for puppies and growing dogs. It is good to administer them after a brief cooking.

FISH:

It is more appetizing when cooked. It is an excellent source of well-digestible proteins and high biological value. It is also rich in minerals and vitamins. Its administration is recommended for

A Comprehensive Guide to Care, Communication, and Adventures with Your Loyal Companion

growing dogs. Dried fish is also good, especially during winter.

EGGS:

They are excellent foods, rich in high biological value proteins, fats, and vitamins. They are particularly suitable for puppies, breeders, and during lactation. They can partially replace meat and fish and can be administered raw.

MILK:

It is an excellent food that provides high biological value proteins, fats, vitamins, and minerals. It is one of the main foods for puppies. Some adult subjects do not digest it well due to the lack of lactase (specific enzyme).

FATS, LARD, AND VEGETABLE OILS:

Excellent sources of calories, very appetizing to dogs, which tend to eat more than necessary. They are useful for working dogs and those performing physical efforts and are indispensable in a certain quantity. It is advisable to add a little olive oil or seed oil to the ration.

RICE AND PASTA: They are among the main sources of energy as they are rich in starch. They must be well-cooked to be digested.

STALE BREAD: an excellent source of energy, generally well-liked by dogs. It should be dry and left out in the air. It should not be moldy, as it could be harmful.

CEREAL FLAKES AND PUFFED RICE:

they are excellent sources of energy that can replace rice, pasta, and bread. They need to be adjusted to preventively treat them to be well-digested by the dog. They are bulky foods, so their weight, not their volume, should be taken into account when adding them to the ration.

VEGETABLES AND FRUIT:

they have a low nutritional value, but their raw fiber content can be useful for sedentary dogs that tend towards obesity or have constipation. They can be replaced with a few spoonfuls of bran.

BONES:

dogs love them, especially those that can be well-chewed, like the knee. However, care must be taken because, especially in older and sedentary individuals, they can cause constipation or even intestinal obstruction. Bone splinters can cause intestinal perforation. In particular, chicken and rabbit bones should be avoided.

SWEETS AND CHOCOLATE:

dogs are greedy and it is difficult to eat a piece of chocolate without them making a small attack. However, one should not overdo it, as they are often not well-digested and can cause problems. There are replacement biscuits on the market that should also not be overused. WATER: must always be available to your dog.

READY-MADE FOODS

There is a wide range of products on the market specifically designed to be well-liked by dogs, however, it is important to know the various types to use them to the fullest. A careful reading of the label on each food package can provide useful

A Comprehensive Guide to Care, Communication, and Adventures with Your Loyal Companion

information. Excessive consumption of proteins, fats, and vitamins should be avoided as they have negative effects on health. Pay attention to the accumulation of substances contained in various foods, especially vitamins and minerals. There are three types of dog food:

SIMPLE FOODS:

different products of animal or vegetable origin (such as puffed rice).

COMPLETE FOODS:

composed of several products that satisfy the nutritional needs of dogs without the addition of other foods or supplements.

COMPLEMENTARY FOODS:

mixtures that have a high content of certain substances (such as proteins, minerals, etc.), but that must be combined with other foods to satisfy the nutritional needs of the dog. The quality of dog food depends on the raw materials used, formulation, technology treatments, and presentation form (flakes, pellets, expanded, blown, biscuit, etc.) as well as storage. The label shows the production and expiration dates, instructions for use, as well as components, which must be listed in decreasing order of quantity or percentage relative to content. Analytical data must also be reported, informing us about the content of the present nutritional principles (water, crude protein, crude fat, crude fiber, ash). The integration of vitamins and minerals per kg of food should also be indicated. Ready-made foods allow for a formulation of the diet based on the real needs of the dog with a correct ratio of proteins and energy, complete vitamin and mineral integration, and not in excess or deficiency as often happens with home-prepared rations. A good complete integrator dog food for adult dogs should have the following analytical content:

maximum humidity of 13%;

crude protein of 22-25%;

crude fat of 4-8%.

Remember that every dog is an individual and dietary needs may vary. It is always advisable to consult your veterinarian to determine the most appropriate diet for your Labrador, taking into account their specific needs and health conditions.

Providing a proper diet for your Labrador is an important way to ensure their overall health and well-being. By following the guidelines provided in this chapter, you can provide your Labrador with balanced nutrition and contribute to their happiness and longevity.

A Comprehensive Guide to Care, Communication, and Adventures with Your Loyal Companion

CHAPTER 12 - HEALTH AND HYGIENE

Regular veterinary visits: Schedule regular veterinary visits for your Labrador, including routine check-ups, vaccinations, and parasite treatments.

When you buy or receive a dog as a gift, whether it's a puppy or an adult, the first instinct is to cuddle it and show it affection in every way possible. However, we must remember that at the same time, we also become responsible for its health.

There are various diseases and health risks, and it's easy to try to replace the vet by diagnosing and treating the dog in an empirical, rushed, and especially wrong way. It's important that the vet be the reference expert, just as every family has a trusted doctor to entrust their health to. The vet can follow your dog over time with appropriate vaccinations and intervene in cases of illness. The relationship of trust between you and the vet will be fundamental in making correct diagnoses and appropriate therapy. In his absence, for emergencies, you can turn to emergency facilities that can intervene even at night.

Today, in addition to general practitioners, there are also specialists in the clinic of pets, officially recognized. Some of them are experts in specific areas such as cardiology, ophthalmology, traumatology, homeopathy, oncology, and others. However, it's advisable that your vet indicates the specialist to consult on a case-by-case basis.

Anyway, you will be spending most of your time with your new four-legged friend, so observe it carefully during the main moments of the day: feeding, walking, playing, sleeping. You need to try to capture those small behavioral and general variations that will alert you and make you suspect a state of illness. The dog, in some ways, can be considered like a newborn who doesn't have the ability to express his feelings verbally but only attracted to specific behaviors and particular vocalizations. Let's see which general symptoms to pay attention to and, if prolonged, consult the vet.

Although it's a mistake to think that you know all the symptoms and diseases of the dog and believe that you can cure them yourself, it's still important to know when the situation requires a rapid intervention of the vet. Some symptoms are indeed signs of serious illnesses.

Some physiological reference parameters can be useful to evaluate the health status of the dog, which, however, we remember, must be observed at rest. In fact, physical exertion or play can accelerate breathing and heart rate and raise the temperature without it being pathological.

Pay attention to your Labrador's health signs, such as changes in appetite, weight, energy, or mood. If you notice anything unusual, consult your veterinarian.

Ensure that your Labrador receives all recommended vaccinations and preventive treatments for common diseases such as parvovirus, rabies, and leptospirosis.

Finally, spaying or neutering can be considered, discussing with the veterinarian the benefits and specific considerations for your dog.

A Comprehensive Guide to Care, Communication, and Adventures with Your Loyal Companion

CHAPTER 13 - COMMON LABRADOR DISEASES: PREVENTION AND MANAGEMENT

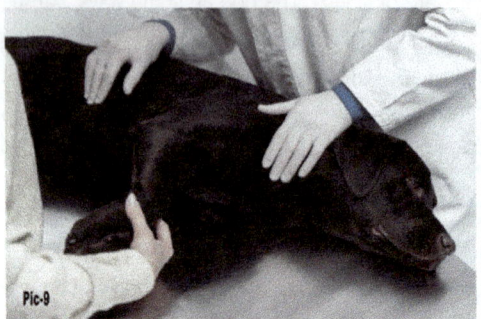

Labradors are generally robust and healthy dogs, but like all breeds, they are susceptible to certain diseases and conditions. In this chapter, we will explore the common diseases that can affect Labradors and provide detailed information on how to prevent and manage them.

By familiarizing yourself with the common diseases that can affect Labrador Retrievers, such as hip dysplasia or diabetes, you can recognize early symptoms and take prompt action.

Taking comprehensive and loving care of your Labrador is essential to ensure a healthy and happy life for your pet. By following the advice and recommended practices in this chapter, you will be able to provide optimal care for your Labrador, meeting their needs for nutrition, exercise, hygiene, and health. Remember to always consult your veterinarian for any health concerns or for further specific advice regarding your dog. Be a responsible and affectionate companion to your Labrador, and you will be rewarded with the love and loyalty of a happy and healthy four-legged friend.

Dogs can suffer from various diseases, many of which, but not all, are specifically of infectious origin. We will emphasize the importance of regular monitoring of your Labrador's health, including periodic veterinary exams, laboratory tests, and signs of alarm that require immediate veterinary attention.

Prevention is crucial for maintaining the health of your Labrador. We will discuss recommended vaccinations, deworming programs, and preventive measures to reduce the risk of exposure to common diseases.

Dogs can suffer from various diseases, many of which, but not all, are specifically of infectious origin.

ORGANIC DISEASES

These are diseases that affect a specific organ or part of it: they have different causes and do not always have the same course; they are not always contagious; their outcome depends directly on the severity of the symptoms.

INFECTIOUS DISEASES

Of viral and bacterial origin; generally affect multiple organs, are contagious, and often fatal; recovery depends on the severity of the symptoms and the dog's immune response; can be prevented with vaccinations.

DISTEMPER: Distemper, is a highly contagious viral disease that affects dogs and other animals,

A Comprehensive Guide to Care, Communication, and Adventures with Your Loyal Companion

such as foxes and raccoons. The disease is caused by the virus of the Paramyxoviridae family.

Distemper is widespread worldwide and can affect dogs of all ages, although puppies and unvaccinated dogs are at higher risk. It has an incubation period of about 3-7 days.

The symptoms of the disease can vary depending on the dog's age, the severity of the infection, and the conditions of the dog's immune system. Symptoms may include fever, lethargy, cough, mucopurulent nasal and eye discharge, diarrhea, vomiting, seizures, paralysis, conjunctivitis with photophobia, cough with lung complications leading to bronchopneumonia, gastroenteritis, very high temperature (41°C) in the first phase of the disease, almost normal during the nervous stage, irreversible damage to the nervous system (paralysis of the hind legs and nervous ticks). The disease is frequently fatal.

Distemper can be diagnosed through blood tests and laboratory tests. At present, there is no specific cure for the disease, but treatment aims to manage symptoms and prevent complications. Furthermore, prevention is essential to protect dogs from Distemper. Vaccination is the most effective way to prevent the disease. Vaccinations usually start when puppies are between 6 and 8 weeks old and are repeated at regular intervals throughout the dog's life.

In conclusion, Distemper is a severe viral disease that can cause serious harm to the health of dogs. Prevention through vaccination is the key to protecting our four-legged friends from this disease. If you suspect that your dog may be infected, it is important to immediately contact a veterinarian for a proper diagnosis and treatment.

INFECTIOUS HEPATITIS: Infectious Hepatitis is a viral disease that affects dogs of all ages with an incubation period of 3 to 9 days; fever at the beginning of the disease; serous conjunctivitis and iridocyclitis; tonsillitis; appearance of very small hemorrhages on the abdominal skin; abdominal tenderness; corneal opacity after 1-3 weeks.

HERPESVIRUS: Canine herpesvirus (CHV) is a virus that affects dogs, especially puppies and newborns, and is almost always lethal. It is a highly contagious virus that can be transmitted through direct contact with an infected dog or contaminated objects, such as food or water bowls. Canine herpesvirus infection can have variable symptoms, but can cause respiratory problems, fever, coughing, sneezing, red and watery eyes, lethargy, and loss of appetite. In puppies, different systems can be affected and symptoms may include diarrhea, vomiting, tracheitis, and neurological symptoms; in adults, the most frequent symptom is laryngotracheobronchitis accompanied by rhinitis; a genital form can occur in both sexes. The infection can be particularly severe and can lead to complications such as pneumonia or death. The virus easily spreads in dog breeding facilities, kennels, and places where dogs come into contact with other dogs. If a dog is suspected to be infected, it is important to isolate the infected dog from others to prevent the spread of the virus. Currently, there is no cure for canine herpesvirus. However, there are treatments available to alleviate symptoms and reduce the severity of the infection. Furthermore, prevention is crucial to prevent the spread of the

A Comprehensive Guide to Care, Communication, and Adventures with Your Loyal Companion

virus. Vaccination of puppies is an important measure to prevent canine herpesvirus infection. In summary, canine herpesvirus is a viral disease that can be severe in puppies. Prevention through vaccination and isolation of infected dogs is important to prevent the spread of the virus. If a dog is suspected to be infected, it is important to immediately consult a veterinarian for proper diagnosis and treatment.

PARVOVIRUS: Canine parvovirus is a highly contagious viral disease that affects dogs of all breeds and ages, but is more common in unvaccinated puppies. The disease is caused by the canine parvovirus, which attacks the cells of the dog's gastrointestinal tract. Symptoms of parvovirus in dogs can vary, but often include bloody diarrhea, vomiting, loss of appetite, fever, lethargy, and dehydration. The disease can be severe and in some cases can lead to the death of the dog. The virus easily spreads through contact with infected feces, even in very small amounts. Puppies and unvaccinated dogs are particularly at risk of contracting the disease, but vaccinated dogs can also contract it in some cases. Prevention is crucial to protect dogs from parvovirus. Vaccination is the most effective way to prevent the disease. Vaccinations against parvovirus generally begin when puppies are between 6 and 8 weeks old and are repeated at regular intervals throughout the dog's life. Additionally, it is important to avoid contact of the dog with infected feces and regularly clean the environment in which it lives. If a dog is suspected to be infected with parvovirus, it is important to immediately contact a veterinarian for proper diagnosis and treatment. Treatment of parvovirus can be costly and demanding, but can save the dog's life if started promptly. Hemorrhagic gastroenteritis, vomiting, dehydration, weight loss, depression, hypothermia, and leukopenia can occur. There is a cardiac form that is generally fatal in puppies.

KENNEL COUGH: Kennel cough, also known as "canine cough", is a highly contagious respiratory disease that affects dogs. It is caused by various pathogens, such as the canine parainfluenza virus and the Bordetella bronchiseptica bacteria. Typical symptoms of kennel cough include a dry and persistent cough, often accompanied by vomiting or regurgitation. Dogs affected by kennel cough may also have a fever, loss of appetite, and lethargy. Kennel cough can be transmitted from dog to dog through direct contact or through respiratory secretions. However, you can protect your dog from kennel cough through vaccination and avoiding contact with infected dogs. If you suspect that your dog may have kennel cough, it is important to consult your veterinarian for appropriate diagnosis and treatment. In many cases, kennel cough can be treated with cough suppressants and antibiotics, if necessary.

RABIES: Rabies is a very serious viral disease that affects mammals, including dogs and humans. It is caused by a virus that attacks the central nervous system of the dog and can lead to fatal neurological symptoms. Rabies in dogs is transmitted through the bite or saliva of an infected animal. It affects many wild and domestic mammals. Symptoms of rabies in dogs can include aggression, bizarre behavior, lethargy, and difficulty swallowing. The nervous system is affected with progressive paralysis; variable behavioral changes; in the dumb form, progressive paralysis of the muscles

A Comprehensive Guide to Care, Communication, and Adventures with Your Loyal Companion

of the jaw, vocal cords, and other muscles of the head with consequent abundant salivation and aphonia, inability to swallow and drink; in the furious form extreme restlessness followed by a hyperexcited state with abundant salivation and howling; death from extensive paralysis; danger of contagion to humans. Since rabies is a highly contagious and dangerous disease for humans, it is important to take necessary precautions to prevent the spread of the disease. Vaccination is the most effective method to prevent rabies in dogs. In many countries, rabies vaccination is mandatory for dogs. In the event of exposure to a potentially infected animal, it is important to immediately consult a veterinarian and, if necessary, initiate post-exposure treatment to prevent the spread of the disease. Rabies in dogs is a very serious and potentially deadly disease, but it can be prevented with vaccination and by taking appropriate precautions to avoid contact with infected animals.

LEISHMANIASIS: Leishmaniasis is a parasitic disease caused by a protozoan called Leishmania, which is transmitted to dogs through the bite of the female sandfly of the genus Phlebotomus, also known as the "sandfly." The disease is endemic in many parts of the world, particularly in Mediterranean regions, Latin America, and some parts of Asia and Africa. Symptoms of leishmaniasis in dogs may include weight loss, hair loss, lethargy, fever, loss of appetite, diarrhea, anemia, swelling of the lymph nodes, skin lesions, and kidney problems. The disease can be difficult to diagnose as symptoms can be similar to those of other diseases. There is no cure for leishmaniasis in dogs, but therapies are available to control symptoms and prevent the progression of the disease. Treatment is usually long-term and involves the use of antiparasitic drugs and supportive therapies. The success of treatment depends on the timeliness of diagnosis and the stage of the disease. Prevention of leishmaniasis in dogs includes protection against sandflies, such as through the use of insect repellents and avoiding exposure outdoors during peak sandfly activity. Additionally, there is a vaccine available for the prevention of leishmaniasis in dogs, which can be administered to dogs in areas where the disease is endemic. In summary, leishmaniasis is a parasitic disease transmitted by sandflies to dogs in many parts of the world. Prevention is important to avoid infection in dogs, and early treatment can improve their health. If you suspect that your dog may have leishmaniasis, consult your veterinarian for appropriate diagnosis and treatment.

LEPTOSPIROSIS: Leptospirosis is a bacterial disease that can affect dogs of all ages, as well as other animals and humans. The mouse and rat are the main sources of contagion; the disease can present with varying degrees of severity. It is caused by bacteria belonging to the genus Leptospira, which are transmitted through the urine of infected animals and can survive in the environment for several weeks. Symptoms of leptospirosis in dogs can vary depending on the severity of the infection, but may include fever, vomiting, diarrhea, loss of appetite, lethargy, increased thirst and urination, joint and muscle pain, jaundice (yellowing of the skin and tissues), and bleeding. Nephritis, conjunctivitis, mild paresis of the hind limbs, gastritis with vomiting, cardiovascular and circulatory deficit, and rarely bronchopneumonia may also occur; the course of the disease can often be fatal.

Leptospirosis in dogs can be diagnosed through blood and urine tests, but early diagnosis can be difficult as symptoms can be similar to those of other diseases. Treatment of leptospirosis in dogs includes the use of antibiotics and supportive therapies to help the dog fight the infection. Leptospirosis in dogs is a potentially serious disease that can be prevented through vaccination. Vaccination against leptospirosis is often recommended for dogs that spend time outdoors, live in areas where the disease is common, or have a high risk of exposure. Additionally, it is important to avoid exposing the dog to the urine of infected animals and to keep the environment clean where the dog lives. In summary, leptospirosis is a bacterial disease that can be transmitted to dogs through the urine of infected animals and can cause severe symptoms. Vaccination and prevention are important to avoid infection in dogs. If you suspect that your dog may have leptospirosis, it is important to consult your veterinarian immediately.

INFESTING DISEASES (PARASITOSIS)

Parasitic diseases are caused by unicellular organisms such as coccidia, or more complex ones like intestinal worms. Parasites live with the dog in a dynamic equilibrium that can lead, in extreme cases of infestation, to the death of the animal. By damaging tissues or depriving the dog of essential nutrients, parasites weaken it and make it more susceptible to infectious diseases.

Infection usually occurs through the ingestion of eggs or larvae introduced into the environment by other sick dogs. Therefore, constant monitoring of one's own dog, in addition to being an obvious advantage for him, is also beneficial for others, reducing environmental contamination. Some parasites are also dangerous to humans, often serving as an intermediate host (e.g. echinococcus tapeworm). Therapies, which we have described here purely indicatively, are based on the parasite and the affected organ. Remember to carefully follow the veterinarian's prescriptions, as the medication may be harmful to the dog.

MYCOSIS

These are diseases caused by microscopic fungi, yeasts, and molds; they are contagious to dogs and humans, especially children (ringworm); adequate environmental and skin hygiene of the dog reduces the risk of contagion; in most cases, they are curable; in the most common forms, they manifest with alopecic areas (hair loss).

CONGENITAL DISEASES

These are present at birth and are caused, for example, by genetic factors or nutritional deficiencies in the mother dog; the affected organs are varied; they are not contagious; they may or may not be compatible with the puppy's life.

HEREDITARY DISEASES

These are diseases caused by particular genes present in the parents and inherited by the puppy; they may manifest at birth or become evident later. The dog can subsequently transmit the same defect to its offspring.

The most well-known ones include hip dysplasia, eye diseases, and hemophilia. In particular, we can pay attention to hip dysplasia, which is a pathology that affects the hip joint and, in the most severe

forms, causes lameness of the hind limbs to a more or less evident degree. The cause is to be found in an altered conformation of the joint with consequent subluxation, wear, and erosion of the cartilage. Degeneration over time leads to phenomena of deforming arthritis. Although the genetic origin has been identified, the transmission mechanism has not yet been clarified. The study of heredity is indeed complex: multiple genes are involved (polygenic character), and their effect can be increased by the environmental conditions of reproduction and growth. The recessive genetic behavior can mask the presence of the trait, which may not appear in the parents and then reappear in the offspring. Some breeds seem to be more predisposed than others. Anatomical construction, both bony and muscular, particularly the width and inclination of the pelvic bones, probably plays an important role. Dysplasia is more easily manifested in subjects with rapid growth. Radiographic examination of the hip joint is now universally accepted as the means to identify affected individuals and those with mild anomalies. The radiograph should be performed by an experienced veterinarian, with the dog under anesthesia to ensure adequate muscle relaxation and thus correct dorsal-ventral positioning of the dog.

 A Comprehensive Guide to Care, Communication, and Adventures with Your Loyal Companion

CHAPTER 14 - FIRST AID FOR LABRADORS: KEEPING YOUR CANINE SAFE AND HEALTHY

The safety and health of your Labrador are top priorities. In this chapter, we will explore the importance of knowing the basic principles of first aid for dogs and provide a detailed guide on how to handle emergency situations and common injuries that may involve your Labrador.

Knowing the signs of emergency: It is crucial to recognize signs of emergency in dogs, such as difficulty breathing, bleeding, and shock. Pay attention to any sudden changes in behavior or health status of your Labrador and take prompt action if you suspect an emergency.

Create a first aid kit for dogs: Prepare a dedicated first aid kit for your Labrador. Make sure to include essentials such as bandages, saline solution for eye irrigation, sterile gauze pads, medical scissors, tweezers for foreign body removal, and emergency veterinary phone numbers.

We will describe some of the most common injuries that may involve Labradors and how to manage them. This includes wounds, cuts, burns, insect bites, allergic reactions, and poisonings. We will provide detailed instructions on how to provide first aid in case of such injuries.

In the event of choking or respiratory distress, it is essential to keep the airways of your Labrador clear of obstructions. You will learn specific airway obstruction clearance techniques and cardiopulmonary resuscitation (CPR) for dogs.

If your Labrador experiences a fracture or trauma, it is important to stabilize the affected area and safely transport the dog to the veterinarian. We will provide instructions on how to temporarily immobilize a fracture and manage traumatic injuries.

Intoxications and poisonings: Labradors can be curious and prone to ingesting toxic substances. We will guide you on how to recognize signs of poisoning and what immediate measures to take if poisoning is suspected.

A Comprehensive Guide to Care, Communication, and Adventures with Your Loyal Companion

In emergency situations or in the case of chronic illnesses, you may need to administer medication to your Labrador. You will learn the correct techniques for administering oral medications, injections, and managing prescribed medications from the veterinarian.

Remember that first aid is a temporary intervention, and it is crucial to always consult a veterinarian for a thorough evaluation and appropriate treatment.

EMERGENCIES SHOCK

- Shock occurs when:
- there is severe cardiocirculatory insufficiency;
- there is peripheral vasodilation;
- there is accumulation of toxic substances in the tissues.

CAUSES: severe trauma; hemorrhages; anaphylactic reactions; cardiac and neurological diseases; toxicosis and dehydration; electric shocks.

SYMPTOMS: pale mucous membranes; strong depression; decrease in body temperature and muscle tremors; small and frequent pulse; shortness of breath; soft feces and urine; vomiting; collapse.

WHAT TO DO: keep the dog warm and calm; immediately consult a veterinarian for possible intravenous infusion or plasma transfusion, administration of anti-shock drugs, painkillers, analgesics, and oxygen. The dog should be monitored for a few days to ensure that the phenomenon has been completely overcome.

POISONINGS

They can be accidental or intentional. If you notice that the dog has ingested dangerous substances, you can induce vomiting by giving him half a glass of water in which a tablespoon of salt has been dissolved or by stimulating the palate and throat. These maneuvers should be avoided if the dog has ingested strong acids or alkalis or harmful objects.

To avoid intentional poisonings, it is necessary to teach your dog to refuse food offered by strangers and discarded food. To avoid accidental poisonings, common sense measures are sufficient.

How to avoid accidental poisoning:

• Avoid letting the dog ingest shampoo and antiparasitic products during treatments.

• Prevent the dog from wandering freely in cellars and courtyards where pest control treatments have recently been carried out. • Keep all medicines, poisonous substances, and household chemicals out of the reach of dogs.

• Do not store dangerous products together with food.

• Do not leave medicines within reach of dogs, especially if they are puppies.

• Do not leave food or water bowls in the garden during pest control treatments.

• Promptly remove dead animals from courtyards and gardens.

INSECT STINGS

Dogs are often stung on the head by bees, wasps, horseflies, etc. Although painful, the stings have transient effects, sometimes even mild. Usually, it is sufficient to cool the area with plenty of water and administer antihistamines orally. The situation can be more serious when the dog is stung behind the throat while attempting to eat the insect. In this case, the swelling reaction can be intense, and the risk of severe suffocation. Immediately consult a veterinarian, and if not possible, in extreme cases, administer antihistamines intravenously (injection). Also, in the case of multiple stings, immediately go to the veterinarian, who can intervene before an anaphylactic shock develops.

To prevent infestations, use veterinarian-recommended anti-parasitic products to protect your Labrador from fleas, ticks, and other external parasites.

SNAKEBITE

The muzzle is the most exposed part, generally bitten during the attempt to capture. If the dog is in good health, it can overcome the poisoning, which nevertheless requires treatment with antivenom serum and veterinary assistance.

HEATSTROKE

Pic-10

It usually occurs during the summer or hot seasons, especially when the dog is left in a car with closed windows. To maintain its body temperature, the dog generally comes into contact with cool and shady surfaces, not being able to increase lung ventilation, which, however, sometimes is not sufficient. The evident symptoms are staggering, a considerable increase in rectal temperature, warm and dry skin, frequent pulse, dyspnea, collapse, death. In the presence of such symptoms, try to lower the body temperature by wetting the dog with cold water, keeping it at rest in a cool and shaded place. Call the veterinarian urgently.

FRACTURES

The most frequent fractures are generally those of the limbs, spine, and jaw. Usually, they result from violent traumas such as road collisions or falls from heights. They can affect one or more bones and, in the most severe cases, the stumps may protrude from the wound (open fracture). The symptoms are limping with severe pain, swelling, bleeding, paresis or paralysis, and, in the most severe cases, a state of shock. In this case, leave the dog as calm as possible, giving it time to recover from the shock and adapt to acute pain. In the case of broken limbs, try to move them as little as possible, and if the veterinarian's intervention cannot be immediate, temporarily immobilize the limb with wooden or cardboard splints and bandages. Always clean and disinfect infected wounds, then cover them with a gauze. If the dog cannot move, lay it on the ground and transport it to the veterinarian with the help of a towel, being careful not to stress the spine. An accurate veterinary examination with radiological analyses is always advisable

A Comprehensive Guide to Care, Communication, and Adventures with Your Loyal Companion

even in cases of mild trauma and poor symptomatology, as mild fractures, if neglected, cannot be the cause of permanent anomalies.

FIRST AID TIPS

SYMPTOMS OF SERIOUS ILLNESSES

• Slow, fast, irregular, or shallow breathing and heart rate

• Low (hypothermia) or high (fever) body temperature

• Melena (presence of blood in feces)

• Hematuria (presence of blood in urine)

• Hematemesis (vomiting blood)

• Epistaxis (nosebleed)

GENERAL SYMPTOMS OF ILLNESS

• Lethargy • Depression

• Refusal to play

• Lack of appetite (anorexia)

• Persistent vomiting and/or diarrhea

• Nasal and/or conjunctival discharge

• Unexplained thirst and/or hunger

• Noticeable weight loss • Dull coat

HOW TO MEASURE BODY TEMPERATURE

Many owners suspect a fever by observing the dog's nose: if it is not wet and cool, they think the dog has a fever. This is not always true. In any case, it is best to measure rectal temperature using a veterinary or pediatric thermometer lubricated with oil or vaseline cream. Lift the tail and gently insert the thermometer (2-3 cm) using a twisting motion, and wait for about 3 minutes.

HOW TO MEASURE HEART RATE

It is possible to place your ear directly against the chest to perceive the heartbeat. Alternatively, the pulsations of the femoral artery can be detected by pressing the outer surface of the thigh with the thumb and the inner surface simultaneously with the index and middle fingers. The artery will now be gently pressed against the femur, and you will be able to feel the pulse.

WHAT TO KEEP FOR EMERGENCIES

• Disinfectants: hydrogen peroxide, iodine tincture, mercurochrome.

• Mild solutions and disinfectants: saline solution, boric water.

• Intestinal astringents and antibiotics.

• Laxatives: vaseline oil.

• Antiemetics.

• An emergency antibiotic recommended by the veterinarian.

• Gauze pads, adhesive tape, 5 cm gauze for dressings.

• The phone number of the trusted veterinarian.

HOW TO BEHAVE WITH A TRAUMATIZED DOG

A traumatized dog, often hit by a vehicle, is usually very scared and disoriented. Therefore, it is important to approach it cautiously to avoid increasing its fear and causing it to run away, perhaps towards escape routes that are unreachable by the rescuer. Speak to the dog in a calm voice and try to reassure it rather than forcing it to stop. If the trauma was particularly violent, the dog may be in shock and experience severe pain from fractures and contusions. In this case, approach slowly and speak calmly, as the dog will recognize the tone of your voice and be reassured. Do not make sudden movements and be careful because the fear and pain may make the dog particularly irritable and aggressive. In response to your care, you may risk getting bitten. If necessary, put a muzzle or an emergency leash on it before moving or lifting it. Try to remain calm because the dog will certainly perceive your tension, which will increase its irritability. Help it with gentleness to avoid worsening the traumas it has suffered and have it checked by a veterinarian or emergency center as soon as possible.

HOW TO TRANSPORT A TRAUMATIZED DOG

If the dog is not able to get up and walk on its own, you should try to lift it in the least traumatic way possible. Large dogs can be transported on emergency stretchers, such as a blanket, coat, or sheet whose four corners serve as handles. Make as few movements as possible, and if the hind legs seem completely paralyzed, suspect a spinal cord injury. In this case, try not to bend the spine in dangerous positions to recover spinal cord function.

HOW TO DEAL WITH A WOUND

It is not possible to treat the various wounds that a dog can get while playing, working, or sometimes even eating, specifically. However, some general rules may be helpful.

The first rule is to stop the bleeding by compressing the area of the wound with a clean handkerchief or sheet. If there is intense bleeding, such as in wounds to the legs, try to stop it by applying pressure above the cut. You will immediately notice that the flow decreases. Use a belt, string, or leash as a hemostatic bandage, which you will tighten to the point where you can loosen the grip occasionally (every 10 minutes) to allow some blood to circulate in the leg. If the wound is in the abdomen or chest, try to apply compression with a towel or folded sheet. In most cases, this will stop the bleeding, but sometimes the veterinarian needs to suture the severed blood vessel to definitively stop the bleeding.

The second intervention is to thoroughly disinfect the wound and try to remove dirt and debris. Be careful, as an irritated dog may bite you; muzzle it before proceeding. Apply a provisional gauze over the clean and disinfected wound to prevent further contamination and go to the veterinarian to assess the real damage. In wounds to the limbs, tendons and nerves may also be affected and must be sutured quickly to avoid permanent damage. If the wound is that of an exposed fracture, try to wash it with saline solution and hydrogen peroxide, cover it with a gauze and go immediately to the veterinarian. The injured tissues are easily infected, and very difficult diseases to cure may arise (osteomyelitis).

INJURIES TO EYES, EARS, NOSE

A Comprehensive Guide to Care, Communication, and Adventures with Your Loyal Companion

Cat and dog scratches can cause serious corneal injuries. Equally dangerous is violent trauma that can cause the eyeball to protrude from the socket. In all cases, wash the injured eye with saline solution, boric acid solution, or clean water; keep the protruding eye moist with a wet cloth and seek veterinary care immediately. Be careful as eye injuries are very painful.

The most common injury to the ears is a laceration or bleeding wound, or an internal hematoma in the ear flap. In both cases, try to stop the bleeding by compressing the affected area, perhaps by bending the ear over the head and applying ice. Consult a veterinarian as soon as possible.

Nosebleeds are perhaps the most distressing for the owner. Generally, dogs can feel the blood flowing out of their nostrils and sneeze, throwing red droplets all around. Nosebleeds can be caused by poisoning or small foreign bodies that have entered the nose and damaged a small blood vessel, creating a strong irritation that makes the dog sneeze violently. Try to stop the bleeding with ice packs and go to the veterinarian.

BURNS

Burns in dogs are not very common, at least those caused by fire, given their innate instinct to stay away from it. However, there may be other causes such as boiling water in a pot on the stove with meat, or scorching chemicals that accidentally fall on them. As a first aid measure, wash with plenty of cold water that will remove the irritating substance and immediately cool the affected area in case of heat burns. Prepare cold compresses to keep on the affected area to reduce vasodilation.

Cover the burn and go to the veterinarian, who will check for shock that may occur as a result of extensive burns.

FREEZING

In our climates, it is not a frequent phenomenon, but it can occur in the mountains. Generally, the limbs and the tips of the ears are affected. Take the animal to a heated environment and cover it to raise its temperature. Gently massage the frozen parts and try to warm them with warm clothes or hot water bags. A pinkish color of the skin will indicate the restoration of circulation.

CHOKING

It is an emergency that requires prompt intervention. Keep the dog's mouth open, as it is already trying to remove the foreign object, lower its tongue and look at the back of its throat. If you can see the foreign object, remove it. To avoid being bitten, gently hold a bit of the lip between the teeth; this will prevent the dog from closing its jaws. If you don't see anything and the dog is too heavy to be lifted by its hind legs and shaken to dislodge the foreign body, give firm but not too violent blows to the chest: the expelled air may dislodge the obstructing object.

CONVULSIVE AND EXCITATORY CRISES

Usually, a convulsive seizure can be frightening for the owner, especially if it is particularly intense. In these circumstances, try to keep the dog in an area without sharp corners where it could hurt itself during the convulsive or excitatory phase. Once the seizure has passed, leave the animal quiet in a room, limiting noise and light until it has fully recovered; cover it with a blanket. When the seizure is completely over (usually lasting a few minutes), take the dog to the veterinarian.

HOW TO ADMINISTER MEDICATIONS

Unfortunately, a sick dog is already an irritable subject and is not always willing to willingly take medication. Therefore, the first attempt should be made with cunning, the second with decision. Oral medications come in different types, but for convenience, we can divide them into tablets, capsules, lozenges, etc., and liquid medications. For the first type, you can try to administer it with a small amount of food, hiding the taste with a food that the dog particularly likes (cheese, meat). In the case of powders or crushed pills, you can try to mix them with a bit of meat, giving the rest of the meal after making sure that the dog has eaten all the first portion. However, there are cases where the medication cannot be mixed with food because it could spoil, or because it has such a strong taste that it is recognized by the dog and therefore refused. In this case, open the dog's mouth, insert the tablet deep down, closing it quickly, and, holding the head up, massage the throat to stimulate swallowing. Make sure your dog has swallowed the medicine, as sometimes it holds the pill in the corner of its mouth and spits it out as soon as you turn around. Liquid medications can be administered with syringes without a needle, rubber bulbs, or droppers. Keep the head raised, insert the syringe into the corner of the mouth between the lips, and slowly allow the product to flow to enable you to swallow it. Never administer liquids by forcefully holding the mouth open: preventing swallowing could cause choking.

MEDICATIONS FOR PARENTERAL USE

This type of medication is administered by injections made under the skin, into a muscle, or a vein. The owner should learn to perform subcutaneous injections to continue the therapies prescribed by the veterinarian, always using single-use or sterilized syringes. A fold of skin should be raised along the back between the neck and the flank, disinfect the skin by lifting the hair and insert the tip of the needle parallel to the spine. Then inject the medication. If the product is irritating, get help from another person to hold the dog still.

MEDICATIONS FOR EAR INFECTIONS

Raise the tip of the ear and insert the dropper into the ear canal. Let the drops fall, then massage the bottom to distribute the product evenly. Keep the dog's head lowered for a few minutes, or it will shake to get rid of the medication that irritates its ear.

DRUGS FOR EYES

Hold the dog's head up and let the eye drops drip onto the cornea. If you need to administer ointment instead, lower the lower eyelid and put some ointment on the inside of the eyelid. Let the eye close again and massage it to distribute the ointment evenly. Remove any excess on the outside with a tissue.

SUPPOSITORIES

A Comprehensive Guide to Care, Communication, and Adventures with Your Loyal Companion

The use of suppositories in dogs is not very common, but it may be necessary to relieve acute pain. In this case, moisten the suppository with water, lift the dog's tail and gently and slowly insert the product without force. Push the suppository deep, perhaps with the help of a cotton swab, and hold the tail down on the perianal area for a few minutes to prevent the dog from immediately expelling the medication

Taking care of Labradors means being prepared to handle emergency situations and provide timely first aid. Knowing the basic principles of first aid for dogs will give you the confidence and skills necessary to keep your Labrador safe and healthy in case of an emergency.

A Comprehensive Guide to Care, Communication, and Adventures with Your Loyal Companion

CHAPTER 15 - OUTDOOR ADVENTURES WITH YOUR LABRADOR

One of the distinctive traits of Labrador Retrievers is their love for outdoor activities. In this chapter, we will explore the outdoor adventures you can enjoy with your faithful Labrador companion. From leisurely walks to thrilling excursions, you will discover how to make the most of your dog's innate desire to explore the great outdoors.

Nature walks are a perfect way to spend time with your Labrador and immerse yourself in the beauty of nature. Choose trails that offer interesting and stimulating landscapes for your dog. During the walk, allow your Labrador to explore the surrounding environment, sniffing and discovering new scents. Make sure to bring fresh water with you to keep your dog hydrated along the way.

If you're an adventure enthusiast, you may want to take your Labrador on more challenging hikes. Before embarking on a hike, make sure to plan the route and familiarize yourself with the rules of the park or natural area you intend to visit. Ensure you have the necessary equipment, such as a sturdy leash, a secure harness, and a first aid kit for dogs. During the hike, consider your dog's endurance level and take regular breaks to allow them to rest and hydrate.

Labradors are known for their energy and stamina, which makes them excellent companions for activities like jogging. Before starting to run with your dog, ensure they are properly trained on the leash and have completed their bone and muscle growth. Begin with short running sessions and gradually increase the distance and intensity. Pay attention to your dog's heat and fatigue during physical activity and take frequent breaks to allow them to relax and cool down.

Labradors love to play, and the great outdoors offer a wide range of possibilities for fun together. Ball retrieval is one of the favorite games for Labradors. Throw a ball for them to run, grab, and bring back to you. You can also try playing frisbee with your Labrador, making sure to use a frisbee specifically designed for dogs. If you have access to a safe swimming area, let your dog experience the joy of swimming and cooling off on hot days.

Safety is paramount during outdoor adventures with your Labrador. Make sure to keep your dog under control and respect the rules of the area you're in. Check for potential hazards, such as toxic plants or wildlife, and keep your dog safe from dangerous situations. Ensure your Labrador wears a collar with an updated identification tag in case they get lost during the excursion.

Outdoor adventures with your Labrador offer not only fun and joy but also a way to build a stronger bond with your faithful friend. Harness your dog's energy and enthusiasm to explore new places, engage in physical activities, and enjoy the beauty of nature together. Always remember to consider your Labrador's abilities and limitations, ensuring they are adequately trained and protected during outdoor activities.

A Comprehensive Guide to Care, Communication, and Adventures with Your Loyal Companion

CHAPTER 16 - TRAINING TIPS AND TRICKS FOR A HAPPY LABRADOR FAMILY

With proper training, you can promote positive behavior, develop effective communication with your dog, and establish a deep connection based on mutual trust. Take the time to dedicate yourself to training your Labrador and enjoy the lasting results you will achieve.

Training a good retriever is like building a house of cards, only if the foundation is solid can you hope to reach great heights. If the basic obedience is already shaky, the house will easily collapse.

BASIC OBEDIENCE

Start with basic commands: Sit, Stay, Come. These fundamental commands help establish control and cooperation with your Labrador.

Reward your dog with praise, petting, and treats to encourage desired behaviors and make training a positive experience.

Maintain consistency in applying commands and rules to avoid confusion in your Labrador and promote more effective learning.

Introduce your Labrador to a variety of people, animals, and situations from an early age. This early socialization will contribute to developing a confident and well-adjusted dog.

Manage unwanted behavior: Learn to recognize signs of discomfort in your Labrador and adopt management strategies such as crate training and providing appropriate toys to prevent damage to the house or furniture.

It is not necessary to have a robot by your side, a few basic rules are enough:

1. Walk correctly on the leash.
2. Immediately return to the owner when called.
3. Sit or lie down on command.
4. Stay still where left with the "stay" or "stop" command.

After establishing the basics, you can teach your Labrador advanced commands like "Stay" at a distance, "Leave it," and "Retrieve" to enrich their abilities.

Try mental stimulation activities: In addition to traditional training, provide your Labrador with games and mental stimulation activities to challenge their intelligence and keep them mentally active.

Problem-solving and challenge management:

Address common challenges: Discuss strategies for managing common issues such as excessive barking, pulling on the leash, or tendency to dig in the garden.

Create routines and structure: Labradors appreciate a clear routine and daily structure that helps them feel secure and manage their behavior more balanced.

Tips for training in families with children:

Train both the Labrador and the children to respect each other, establishing clear rules and promoting safe and positive interactions.

A Comprehensive Guide to Care, Communication, and Adventures with Your Loyal Companion

Teach children how to interact properly with the dog, involving them in training and engaging them in Labrador's care.

Whether you want a hunting, ring, or companion dog, basic obedience is of fundamental importance: having complete control over your animal is not only useful in relationships with others, to respect the rules of civilized coexistence, but it can also save their life in case of danger.

Every dog should be educated and trained in such a way as not to cause disturbance, harassment, or threats, neither at home nor in a public environment. This way they can follow their owner everywhere without arousing complaints. Your Labrador, once trained, will never give you any problems, in any place or situation you find yourself in, and your bond with them could become even stronger.

Teaching basic rules can begin as soon as you bring your puppy home. The first stages will consist of teaching them where to do their business and where they absolutely cannot, what they can play with and what they cannot, what their name is and which call they must respond to, where their bed is and where they should not climb, etc.

From a young age, your Labrador will learn what "NO!" means. A "NO" said at the right moment is immediately understood and serves much more than any punishment. Learn to communicate with your dog simply with your tone of voice and with some visible gestures, without hitting, slapping, or hitting them with a newspaper on the nose.

It is very important to praise them extensively when they obey or do the right thing. The Labrador puppy is very sociable and sensitive to cooing and compliments, so to reinforce positive behavior, it is sufficient to show enthusiasm and reward them by playing with them, throwing their ball, or doing other things they enjoy. Even a natural reward, such as a dog biscuit, can be useful if given at the right time, although it should not become a habit.

Now let's see what the main rules our dog should learn are:

OBEYING THE RECALL: at any moment and whatever the dog is doing, it must respond to the owner's recall. It is important to get the dog used to a single command, usually the dog's name followed by the word "come" or "here" or "heel" etc. The retriever puppy, being naturally very sociable, will willingly respond to the recall from the beginning, but you will notice that if it is engaged in some activity that particularly interests it, it will not always obey immediately. For this reason, it is useful to praise him effusively when he comes to you and especially not to immediately "catch" him. The leash may not be tolerated by the puppy, so calling him and tying him up immediately can become counterproductive. If you are at home or in your garden, you can repeat the recall exercise more than once, and every time the dog obeys you, reward him. This is the first, simpler phase; later you can start the exercise outdoors. Leave the dog free in a safe place, and after letting him explore a bit, start with the recall, which must always be joyful, never like an imperative order, in the early stages. Repeat the exercise several times and only at the end put the leash back on. Once the puppy has learned its name and responds quickly enough, the recall should be strengthened in increasingly difficult situations. One very important thing to keep in

A Comprehensive Guide to Care, Communication, and Adventures with Your Loyal Companion

mind is that you should never put yourself in a position where you can "lose". If your dog is engaged in a wild game with another dog or is having fun like crazy in a pond, avoid calling him if you think he will not obey. A well-trained adult dog must obey, especially in situations like these, but you cannot expect a young and lively puppy to do so. Also, calling him unnecessarily would only make you nervous, and you would probably end up scolding him harshly as soon as he comes into view. Another thing you should never do is try to go and get the dog. He should always come to you. Being chased is interpreted as a game by your puppy, and in this case, too, you run the risk of losing your patience and punishing him when you catch him, which will make him increasingly distrustful of your call. In fact, he does not understand the reason for the punishment, he cannot associate the flight with the scolding, he simply associates owner + recall = "beating" and the next time it will be harder to make him obey your command. The best method, which requires a lot of patience, is to move away from the dog and continue to call him until he decides to come; praise and caress him and let him go free again. Repeat the exercise two or three times for each problem, until he has learned to respond promptly. The faster he comes to you, the more fun you should give him, so that it is always a joy for him to return to his owner. Walking on the leash is another important part of basic training; the dog must learn to walk beside the owner's left foot, accommodating changes in gait and avoiding both pulling and falling behind. At each stop, the owner should also learn to sit. The collar is put on the puppy around two and a half months, when he will start going out for his first walks. The first few times you will have to pull him because feeling tied up will inevitably block him. In this phase, never give abrupt pulls, make sure the collar and leash cause him as little discomfort as possible. You will see that after the first few times, when the dog sits down and refuses to take another step, or scratches furiously to free himself from the collar, things will slowly improve.

You need to be patient and give him time to get used to it. It would be helpful if two people accompanied him the first few times: one calls the dog to him, the other holds him on the leash. The latter should only lengthen the leash when the dog runs too far ahead and should be gentle if the puppy is close to you. Teaching him to heel should exploit the principle that the dog feels uncomfortable when he moves away from his owner and does not feel hindered when he stays very close to the foot. Once he has become familiar with the leash and accustomed to being tied up, you can begin to teach him how to walk. Using a "slip collar," which tightens when the leash is pulled, you start walking by giving the command "heel," "foot," or "stay close," preceded by the dog's name. If he does it, he stays by your side without pulling, but if he starts to pull, you must give a tug on the leash and repeat the command.

It is not necessary to give powerful tugs, a gentle pull to the right is enough. The exercise must be repeated several times to achieve a perfect gait, but generally, the dog will learn in a short time to walk close to you without pulling. Finally, it will be essential for the hunting dog to behave at heel without a leash. With this exercise, the dog must learn to walk beside you as if he were tied up. The first few times won't be easy, but if you proceed gradually, alternating frequently between behaviors on the leash, the dog will soon learn. "Stay" is another important command that must be preceded by "sit down" or "down"; the dog must learn to stay where you put him, even if you move away or even disappear from his sight. It is a useful command both during hunting, as it allows you to stop the dog until the moment he needs to intervene, but also in everyday life when you need to make your friend wait somewhere.

You start by making him sit or crouch on the ground and give him the command "stay" or "rest," without looking him in the eyes, with a firm but not threatening voice. The command can also be reinforced by raising a hand. You then move away from the dog slowly while continuing to repeat "stay," and after a few meters, you return to him. If he hasn't moved, once you get back to the dog, you congratulate him by petting him; if, on the other hand, he got up to follow you or, worse, got distracted by something else, you need to say a firm "NO!" and put him back where he was. The exercise should be continued by gradually increasing the distance, until you disappear from the dog's sight, or by extending the time during which he must remain still. In this case, too, a lot of patience is necessary, and you should not be in a hurry to achieve a perfect result in a short time.

Most retriever puppies love water, but the first impact is not always easy: even if he feels attracted instinctively, sometimes the dog may have some fear. To help him overcome this phase, you can enter the water yourself and call him; if the season doesn't allow it, you can set a good example with an adult dog that enters the water in front of him, or you can encourage him by throwing something into shallow water. The dog should never, under any circumstances, be forced to enter, as this could scare him even more.

Training your Labrador Retriever is an exciting and rewarding journey. By following the tips and techniques presented in this chapter, you will be able to develop a strong and respectful relationship with your dog, creating a happy and harmonious Labrador family. Remember to be patient, consistent, and dedicate time and effort to the training of your Labrador, and you will be rewarded with a loyal and well-behaved companion.
Always remember to adapt the training to the specific needs of your Labrador and consult a professional trainer or veterinarian if you encounter challenges or persistent behavioral issues.
Wishing you successful training and enjoyment in creating a happy and well-trained Labrador family!

HUNTING TRAINING

Regarding the work of retrieving, there are numerous specific exercises with varying degrees of difficulty that can be carried out during training. It is not the case to go into the details of this subject here, as it would go beyond what a trainer could cover. However, some fundamental rules can be recalled: first of all, it should be kept in mind that it takes two and a half to three years to obtain a good retriever, and there should be no temptation to proceed too quickly even if the dog works well and gives us many satisfactions.

Training must always be gradual; it is wrong to want to put the dog to the test with complicated exercises when basic ones are not yet executed perfectly: he may succeed, but if he fails and escapes your control, you will have taken a step back instead of an improvement. Training should also be constant, but short; the dog cannot concentrate for more than fifteen or twenty minutes. Taking longer lessons is, therefore, a waste of time. All hunting training is based on the ability to control the dog at a distance. To do this, it is necessary to teach him commands by associating a gesture, such as a raised hand or a whistle sound, that can be perceived from afar. The dog will learn to stop, sit on command, and the distance will gradually increase until it reaches considerable lengths. Even the recall to heel must be as precise as possible.

Another fundamental principle that the dog must learn is to start only if requested: he must, therefore, be used to seeing objects fall in front of him, to seeing the dummies thrown, or any other movement, while remaining still in his place. In the early stages of training, therefore, it is better not to be tempted to make the dog retrieve; as a general rule, it is best to allow a maximum of one retrieve per "lesson," even if during the same session, the dummy has been thrown several times. The retriever's instinct would be to run immediately towards the object to be retrieved, but in a hunting expedition, it is fundamental that he knows how to stay in his place without disturbing until it is his turn to intervene. He must be indifferent to movement, confusion, and the "euphoria" encountered during hunting activity; he must know how to distinguish between many words or gestures that do not concern him from those expressly addressed to him. To do this, you must always be careful to give clear commands both with your voice and with gestures. It is not necessary to shout or whistle too loudly; the only thing you need to take care of is the "comprehensibility" of your command. The whistle can also be used quietly; in this way, if you need to reinforce a command, you will only need to increase the intensity of the recall, and the effect will be more immediate.

Another fundamental point is to vary the exercises and the sequence of commands to avoid boring the dog. In each session, all the commands must be passed and repeated more than once before introducing something new, but try to introduce variations in the exercises already known to the dog so that no harmful habits are created.

Getting used to the sound of the gun is done with the help of a person who is at a certain distance while you are close to the dog and reassuring him. We start by making a shot heard from about 150 meters away, followed by others gradually getting closer; if the dog does not show any fear, we can proceed further, but if he shows some concern or intimidation, it is better to stop and try again another day, always starting from afar. Introducing the habit of stopping and sitting at the sound of the gun will happen later, when the dog has become accustomed to the noise and considers it normal.

Blind retrieve is a fundamental exercise that should be performed in the advanced phase, when the dog has been trained to follow the direction indicated by the handler in the search. It consists of sending the dog to search for a dummy previously placed in a more or less hidden location. The dog

A Comprehensive Guide to Care, Communication, and Adventures with Your Loyal Companion

must then be able to find an object that it has not seen fall and of which it does not know the existence simply based on the invitation given by the

handler in the direction in which it must search and on its sense of smell.

I would add that it is difficult for a novice to improvise as a trainer: it is very useful, instead, to rely on an expert, perhaps by following a training course with your own dog, in order to lay the foundations that can then be developed by the owner with constant work.

 A Comprehensive Guide to Care, Communication, and Adventures with Your Loyal Companion

CHAPTER 17 - DOG SHOWS

Dog shows are a competitive activity in which dogs are judged by experts based on their adherence to breed standards and their appearance, movement, temperament, and more. They are divided into classes by age, gender, and any titles, and compete against each other in front of a judge to obtain various qualifications, which depend on the type of show and how many dogs are present.

The judgment is formulated on the beauty and external conformation of the dog in relation to the official standard of the breed to which it belongs. The absolute value of the dog is expressed with a written comment from the judge, which is then summarized in a final qualification.

If you are thinking of participating in dog shows with your dog, here are some tricks and rules to follow and know. Here are some specific tricks and rules for a Labrador Retriever participating in a dog show:

TRAINING: Your Labrador Retriever should be trained to respond to commands, walk and stand correctly during the show. There are specific training courses for the show that you can attend to improve your skills and those of your dog.

GROOMING: The care of the Labrador Retriever's coat is important for the show. You should regularly comb and brush your dog's coat to maintain its natural shine. Also, it is important to cut your dog's nails and clean its ears properly.

HEALTH: Make sure your Labrador Retriever is in good health before participating in a show. Unhealthy dogs will not be allowed in the show, and you should never put your dog's health at risk to participate in a show.

Equipment: Make sure you have everything you need for the show, such as leads, collars, brushes, combs, and products for the care of your Labrador Retriever's coat. Also, bringing a bowl for water and some food for your dog is always a good idea.

REGULATIONS: It is important to know the regulations of the show, including rules of behavior, registration requirements, costs, and restrictions for your Labrador Retriever's participation. Make sure to comply with all rules and have all required documents.

Behavior: Your Labrador Retriever should be well-behaved and act appropriately during the show. Make sure to keep your dog under control and respect the needs of other participants. Also, your Labrador Retriever should be friendly and playful, demonstrating the friendly and sociable character that characterizes them.

ETIQUETTE: Always respect the show etiquettes, such as not touching other dogs without the owner's permission, not speaking during evaluations, and not interfering with the judges. Additionally, it is important to respect other participants and their dogs by showing a respectful and professional attitude.

In summary, participating in a dog show requires preparation, knowledge, and respect for the rules and etiquettes. With proper training, careful grooming, and good health, your Labrador

Retriever can participate in dog shows with success and enjoyment.

The following qualifications are assigned in recognized shows:

EXCELLENT: This is the highest qualification and is awarded to those dogs that come closest to the ideal breed standard, are in perfect condition, and have a harmonious and balanced appearance overall. They must have a brilliant gait, a certain "class," and, most importantly, the clearly evident characteristics of their sex.

Very good: This is awarded to dogs that are perfectly in type, in good physical condition, and overall balanced and harmonious. Some venial defects are tolerated but not morphological ones. In any case, this qualification can only be awarded to a high-quality dog.

Good: This is the judgment given to dogs that possess the characteristics of their breed but have evident defects. The defects must not be disqualifying.

FAIRLY GOOD: This is awarded to dogs that are sufficiently typical but do not have notable qualities or are in poor physical condition.

A show dog must therefore come as close as possible to the breed standard. As for the Labrador, it must have a correct eye color, a double coat with hair and undercoat, a typical head, a sweet expression, good bone structure, and a long tail. If you specify to the breeder at the time of purchase that you intend to take your dog to shows, he or she will advise you on the most promising puppy based on genealogy and morphology. It is not possible to guarantee the future development of a puppy, but someone with an expert eye can certainly guide you correctly.

PREPARATION FOR SHOWS

If you have never participated in a dog show, you can start by attending one to see how you should move in the ring and how to behave with the dog.

It is important to start training the dog at home by walking it on a leash without pulling. Vary the gaits and make it move both in a straight line and in a circle.

In front of a mirror, have the dog stand in the so-called "stand" position, i.e., still in pose. You can attract its attention with biscuits, without letting it sit. It must remain well positioned on all four legs with the dorsal line straight and the tail on the same line, the head erect with a look and ears in an attentive position. Additionally, the dog must be accustomed to being touched by the judge all over the body, opening its mouth to look at the teeth, etc., always remaining still in position.

This type of training should be done gradually and be enjoyable for the dog. Don't force anything on the dog and always set everything up like a game, rewarding it if it behaves well.

The leash used in shows is very simple; it generally consists of a cord ending with a ring that is passed around the dog's neck. This allows the leash to be loosened when the judge looks at your dog and tightened again when the dog is made to walk.

THE FIRST TIME

It is logical that if you choose to participate in an exhibition it will be when you think your dog is in the best physical condition. On the day of the first show, pack everything necessary for the dog in a bag, as you will be spending quite some time inside the exhibition pavilion. Take a blanket for him to lie on, a bowl for water and eventually food, a brush and a soft cloth, a leash, and some biscuits.

Feed your dog the night before, but avoid giving him food on the day of the show to prevent him from feeling sick during the trip. If he is a bit hungry, he will also be more attentive in the ring, hoping to receive some of the biscuits you keep in your pocket.

Usually, cages are available for participants in exhibitions to put their dogs in, but if you have your own cage, it is certainly better to use it.

As soon as you arrive at the show, you will need to pick up the catalog with the list of all the exhibited dogs and an envelope containing your number. Then head towards the ring number indicated for the group (retriever dogs, hunting dogs, and water dogs) and find out about the succession of breeds and classes. If it is not your turn to enter right away, you can let your dog relax by taking a walk and then give him the final touch with a brush and a soft cloth to run over his fur.

When your class is called into the ring, enter calmly and place yourself according to the numbering near the other participants. Write your number on your chest so that it is clearly visible and then follow the directions of the ring secretary who will indicate how to place yourself.

Place the dog in front of you so that the judge can see him from the side, and wait for him to look at all the subjects together. The judge may ask all the participants to take a walk at a steady pace around him and then to increase the pace.

When it's your turn to have your dog examined, approach the judge and place him. Answer any questions the judge may ask about the dog and prepare to have him walk in front of him. Never go too fast, but not too slow either; the dog should have a smooth and harmonious gait next to you. In these stages, the preparation done at home will be very useful.

After the judgment, wait for the judge's decision, and if you are lucky enough to get a good placement the first time, thank the judge and congratulate the other participants. If the result is not as good, do not be discouraged, you can always try again.

THE CLASSES

CHAMPIONS: mandatory for international beauty champions and optional for foreign champions.

OPEN: open to all dogs at least fifteen months old, excluding international beauty champions.

WORKING: for dogs at least fifteen months old and for breeds subjected to work tests.

JUNIOR: intended for dogs aged between nine and eighteen months.

A Comprehensive Guide to Care, Communication, and Adventures with Your Loyal Companion

Thank you so much for choosing to read "Labrador Love" I hope the book has provided you with valuable information and inspiration to take optimal care of your Labrador.

I would like to express my heartfelt gratitude to everyone who contributed to making this book possible. Special thanks to the professionals in the field of dogs and Labrador experts who shared their knowledge and experiences.

I would also like to thank my family and friends for their unwavering support and encouragement throughout the writing process. Without them, this book would not have been possible.

Lastly, I invite you to share your feedback on "Labrador Love" Reader reviews are incredibly important to me and help me improve and provide even more useful content. I encourage you to leave an honest review on the purchase site or dedicated online book platforms.

If you have any questions, comments, or would like further information, please don't hesitate to contact me at daring.limited@gmail.com. I will be happy to respond to your inquiries and provide additional personalized advice.

Thank you again for your support and for choosing **"Labrador Love**" I wish you and your Labrador a life full of happiness, health, and love.

Warm regards,

www.ingramcontent.com/pod-product-compliance
Lightning Source LLC
LaVergne TN
LVHW021944060526
838200LV00042B/1917